CULTURE-LED URBAN REGENERATION IN SOUTH KOREA

by
Milyung Son
The University of Sheffield

Series in Sociology

VERNON PRESS

www.vernonpress.com

In the Americas:
Vernon Press
1000 N West Street, Suite 1200,
Wilmington, Delaware 19801
United States

In the rest of the world:
Vernon Press
C/Sancti Espiritu 17,
Malaga, 29006
Spain

Series in Sociology

Library of Congress Control Number: 2019937907

ISBN: 978-1-64889-299-8

Also available: 978-1-62273-678-2 [Hardback]; 978-1-64889-203-5 [PDF, E-Book]

TABLE OF CONTENTS

Acknowledgements

I am really grateful beyond all description for my family's unwavering courage and unconditional love. Without their unwavering support and prayers, I could not have accomplished this work. In addition, sincere gratitude is given to those participants who contributed their time. Their precise opinions created this book, and I will never forget what they said, their hopes, and their desires. Without their help, this book would be meaningless.

Abbreviations

CCEA	Culture City of East Asia
CCIPF	Cheongju Culture Industry Promotion Foundation
CURTC	Cheongju Urban Regeneration Trust Centre
ECOC	European Capital of Culture
JURC	Jungang Urban Regeneration Committee
KRIHS	Korea Research Institute for Human Settlements
KURC	Korea Urban Regeneration Centre
LCP	Liveable Community Projects
MOLIT	Ministry of Land, Infrastructure and Transport
NURIOs	National Urban Regeneration Intermediary Organisations
SAUR	Special Act on Urban Regeneration
UKCOC	UK City of Culture
URC	Urban Regeneration Centre

List of Figures and Tables

Chapter 1

Introduction

Over the last 30 years, as awareness of urban development has shifted from merely using land sites to deeper spheres such as local economies, social, and environmental priorities, there has been a growing interest in the use of culture and the arts for urban regeneration. A number of positive impacts have emanated from the culture and arts-based approach. For instance, it can increase the consumption of arts and culture in society, be a source of jobs and investment, boost cities' images, build the confidence and skills of local residents, tackle social exclusion, and help community cohesion. In this sense, culture-led urban regeneration schemes have been an important part of tackling urban decline planning in South Korea. A number of local government authorities have invested in cultural infrastructures and programmes to encourage culture-led urban regeneration. Therefore, this book explores the role of culture and arts in regeneration schemes with explanations of the urban regeneration history, recent policies, and practices. To prove the contributions of culture and arts to urban regeneration, social aspects including community development, changes of living or working environment, and personal improvement (e.g. mental health, cultural perspective, and personal skills) – these aspects are regarded as social regeneration in this book - are emphasised. Particularly, it seeks to examine how a year-long cultural event can play an influential role in aspects of social regeneration within declining areas to identify the specific contributions of culture and arts to regeneration. It focuses on the 2015 Culture City of East Asia (hereafter, CCEA) event as a case-study – which commenced in 2014 as a year-long event in small and medium-sized towns of South Korea, China and Japan, and initially followed the aims of the European Capital of Culture event. On the basis of these aims, the key questions of this book are 'how culture-based initiatives support urban regeneration scheme?', and 'have culture-led approaches created social regeneration opportunities?'. To answer those questions, this book comments on the relationships between culture-led urban regeneration initiatives in South Korea and uses a number of local communities' opinions to prove the contribution of culture-led approach to social regeneration impacts. This book is inspired by Landry, Greene, Matarasso and Bianchini, 1996; Matarasso, 1997; Evans and Shaw, 2004; Garcia, Melville and Cox, 2010; and Ennis and Douglass, 2011 and is based on the PhD thesis of the author submitted in 2018 to the University of Sheffield, United Kingdom.

1.1 Debates about Culture and Arts in Urban Regeneration Initiatives

In recent years, the role of culture has been considered to be of unprecedented significance to urban development and has proved to be a means by which to resolve political and socio-economic problems within urban areas (Yudice, 2003). Culture-led regeneration has the distinctive characteristic of integrating cultural elements within urban strategies as culture and embraces design, artworks, cultural activity, music and architecture (Vickery, 2007). As a catalyst of regeneration, the culture-led approach has positively influenced numerous sectors by, for instance, as boosting local economies, improving environmental quality, enhancing community development, and conserving traditional sources of community and local sustainability. This book focuses especially deeply on social regeneration opportunities in which the use of arts and culture "can be a primary empowerment tool utilised by regeneration and neighbourhood renewal practitioners in order to achieve wider regeneration aims based on educational attainment, health, crime and social cohesion" (Northall, n.d., p.3.). Additionally, various art classes or performances such as music, craft, dance, drawing programmes, and so on can play a tacit role in enhancing an individual's literacy and social communication skills, as well as facilitating community cohesion between ages and different cultural backgrounds.

Amongst various approaches within culture-led urban regeneration initiatives, the role of cultural events has attracted growing attention from academics and policymakers over the last 30 years. As cultural event strategies have become key motivations for urban regeneration, their significance has contributed to cultural, economic and social regeneration. As an example, the successful transition of Glasgow in the United Kingdom from a declining industrial city to the European City of Culture (hereafter ECOC) in a YEAR has inspired many local authorities and central governments to utilise cultural events as key drivers of culture-led regeneration. The award of ECOC creates substantial economic and social benefits. Specifically, it is believed that cultural events can stimulate citizen participation to improve cultural provision and create collaborative networks between people within other cultural sectors. Moreover, the positive contributions of cultural events to regeneration may include place promotion, tourism, the creation of new physical and social infrastructure, enhanced employment and training opportunities, increased property values, greater community cohesion, the re-use of redundant buildings, and the use of arts and culture to enhance and improve personal or community well-being.

There are, however, a wide range of tensions between the priorities in culture-led urban regeneration approaches. One notable argument is that many cultural elements within urban regeneration processes have become commercialised, with attention focusing significantly on economic and physical results which bring limited benefits to disadvantaged groups and communities. Overt focus on commercial and private sponsors which can attract large audiences and inward investments may spoil indigenous identities and generate inequality amongst local people and businesses. Some large-sized cultural events enthusiastically pursue selling cities as places for inward investment rather than seeing such events as celebrations of local culture and the life experiences of local citizens. Economic factors are prioritised over unique cultural strategies tailored to local characteristics.

Furthermore, an overtly economic-focused approach can neglect the need for explicit area-based social interventions. The welfare and economic well-being of residents and small businesses, as well as the cohesion of communities, can be excluded. Further controversies over culture-led urban regeneration are discussed in Chapters 2 and 4.

Despite the complicated features of culture-led regeneration initiatives, the use of arts and culture within urban regeneration policies is becoming more important in South Korea. From the 1990s onwards, arts and culture have acted as a catalyst for city marketing policies through the hosting of various local festivals, cultural activities, and the creation of grand-scale cultural facilities. The use of cultural policy and planning has become a key tool of urban development in the metropolitan cities of South Korea. In the early 2000s, the use of culture within urban regeneration started to be expanded and was associated with shifts away from large-scale projects at national or city level to medium and small-sized cultural attempts within local communities. Numerous programmes including festivals, education programmes, and art projects were officially institutionalised by the South Korean central government in 2005, as a means by which to tackle the social problems of declining areas pertaining to dwelling, welfare, work, environment, health, safety, culture, landscape and transportation. This represented an attempt to broaden the impacts of cultural interventions, rather than such programmes merely focusing on economics. In addition, as the top-down approach has significantly proliferated the cultural context of South Korea, bottom-up strategies and the promotion of residents' participation has been actively implemented as a further mechanism by which to address the urban and social problems of disadvantaged areas; discussed in subsequent chapters.

However, there are still ongoing controversies regarding economic-centred cultural interventions such as the contention that they merely build up colossal cultural infrastructures, meaningless mural painting for attracting tourists, inappropriate establishment of a Korea-pop and drama centre in the local areas. These actions focused on economic development, have been criticised for creating result-oriented bureaucracy management with significant tax leakage, the interruption of building construction, the destruction of local characteristics and significant commercialization of culture. Also, the social outcomes including community development, conservation of local historical culture, cultural preferences and social cohesion tended to be ignored. Particularly, Hong (2013) notes that "as culture increasingly becomes a product to be consumed in the global economy, the value of local culture continues to be at risk" (p.29). To tackle such problems, the preservation of local cultures, the balancing of culture versus local economic growth, and the creation of cultural projects with close citizen interaction are desperately needed.

1.2. Rationale for the Research: The Absence of Social Regeneration Research in Culture-led Urban Regeneration.

Despite the proliferation of cultural initiatives aiming to tackle wider social issues, there has been a lack of in-depth research into their actual efficacy. There has been research into one-off events; the cultural policy frameworks of regions; the tourism benefits of cultural investment; and theoretical approaches into culture-led regeneration (Vickery, 2007; McCarthy, 2007; Craggs, 2008). However, there has been little research into the perspectives and experiences of citizens impacted by such initiatives, and there has been little work on community development or personal improvement. The low profile of social research in contemporary culture-led regeneration initiatives reflects the reality that integration with cultural resources and urban policy has been principally evaluated by the outcome of commercial and infrastructural developments. Many pieces of research have questioned the benefits that cultural elements (such as mega-events or signature buildings) can bring to a city? What is the role of culture in economic development? What is the economic valuation of cultural goods and services? How can cultural elements contribute to the growth of tourism and internal investment? This is not to say that such questions should be a major concern in assessing a culture-led urban regeneration strategy. However, the evaluation process of culture-led regeneration frequently fails to ask questions surrounding the 'end impacts' upon communities – Are cultural resources being used to spread culture, or just to enhance economic development? Are the symbolic facilities or mega-events being integrated with the needs of local communities and benefiting local citizens? How can residents consider and shape culture-led regeneration strategies?

In South Korea, there is now an extensive literature concerned with culture-led urban regeneration processes that have dealt with visitors' motivations and the market segmentation of mega-events; the use of cultural facilities after the completion of events; tourism impacts and benefits on the basis of the pre-and post-survey of local residents in a quantitative way; the effects of mega-events on destination images and city branding; the activation of the local economy through cultural event projects, and so on. As emphasised above, the essential purpose of urban regeneration is to offer a better economic and social life, but social impact studies have been neglected.

To address this gap in existent understanding, this book examines how a year-long cultural event played a crucial role in social regeneration within a declining area by focusing on the CCEA in Cheongju, South Korea as a case study. According to published articles, newspapers and evaluation reports, the nature of CCEA made it an ideal vehicle to deliver cultural vibrancy, economic growth, and enhance community solidarity. In terms of urban regeneration, the CCEA increased the city's consumption and culture, and produced an ever-proliferating number of festivals in the city. Since the event in 2014, policy and strategy have been constantly expanded and enriched, and six more cities from within three nations hosted the event in 2016 and 2017. However, there has been a lack of studies examining the actual impacts of the CCEA. By examining the CCEA initiative, this book addresses the role of cultural events in social regeneration by exploring residents' opinions and an understanding of the wider context, in terms of culture-led regeneration within South Korea and the targeted area.

1.3. The Social Dimension of Urban Regeneration

Within many urban regeneration schemes, social dimensions (i.e. enabling people to access opportunities, overcoming multiple deprivations and improving economic opportunities and social well-being) are considered to be important. Ginsburg (1999, p.55) emphasises that "the improved and appropriate delivery of welfare services in poor neighbourhoods and the empowerment of local communities in regeneration process" should be prioritised in social regeneration processes. Usually, social regeneration involves a combination of interventions that focus solely on people (improving skills, health confidence, and education achievement) and/or places (community facilities, better environment, creation of job opportunity, and internal investment). In addition, Ginsburg (1999) and Evans (2005) stress that to achieve successful social regeneration, policies should encompass a variety of social factors – from the initial policy proposal to the final evaluation of the policy's outcomes – including social care for disadvantaged people, the creation of employment and training opportunities. From this, there has been the empowerment of local communities in decision-making processes, and an evaluation of any enhanced levels of investment for neighbourhood civil society. Amongst various social dimensions, this book focuses deeply on community development and living circumstances of local residents through the examination of a case-study which involved 74 respondents (See Appendix 1).

1.4. The Cultural City of East Asia and Its Operation in Cheongju

Historically, South Korea, China and Japan have endured tensions such as conflict, war, colonisation, territorial disputes and enforced sex slavery. This has led to a lack of solidarity and mutual understanding, although they do have close cultural ties (Pre-2014 Asia Culture Forum, 2014). To aid the creation of further ties, the countries have sought to connect their provincial cities through diverse cultural activities. The first step towards cultural integration resulted in a joint statement on 28 September 2013 by the Cultural Ministers of South Korea, China and Japan, that they would be creating a new cultural partnership that would involve the joint programming of performances, exhibitions and multifarious cultural projects. According to this initiative, the 2014 CCEA project was developed to "foster mutual understanding and a sense of unity within East Asia so as to strengthen the international transmission of diverse cultures in the region" through a variety of cultural events (Foreign Press Centre Japan, 2013). The inaugural CCEA was hosted in Gwangju in South Korea, Quanzhou in China, and Yokohama in Japan in 2014.

The CCEA was initially designed to last one year, with the selected city showcasing cultural programmes on an international stage. Primarily, the aim of CCEA is to share a mutual understanding of culture and strengthen a sense of unity by exchanging cultural activities in the region. Cultural events have played a fundamental role in the recent development of European cities, and the initiative aimed to use the CCEA as a powerful instrument for regional regeneration in East Asia. In this sense, 'exchange cultural programmes', 'development and regeneration of provincial cities through cultural programmes', and 'build solidarity in the East Asia region' became the essential purposes of the event (City of Yokohama News Release, 2014). Moreover, as the CCEA benchmarked the ECOC, the initiative hoped to demonstrate the positive ripple effects of culture in vitalising urban regeneration (Gwangju Activity Report, 2015).

Cheongju has long been renowned as a cultural and educational city; its cultural resources epitomise the city's vibrancy. Cheongju was the second CCEA city in 2015 and aimed to reflect the city's aspiration, history and cultural diversity. In 2014, the judges admired Cheongju's great cultural heritage and outstanding plans for 2015's CCEA along with Qingdao in China and Nigata in Japan. The year-long programme showcased its cultural diversity from large-sized festivals and international biennale to small music concerts. By hosting the second CCEA in 2015, Cheongju city received unprecedented national recognition as a city of culture and was given an opportunity to showcase innovative cultural ideas and cultural assets. During the CCEA, the city held, abundant cultural programmes – 27 main events were hosted over a year, and the full CCEA programmes included not only main events, but also exhibition days, performance days, and educational classes. In total, over 70 activities were held in 2015. However, there were criticisms that the approach became top-down (being inherited from the national South Korean Government) and local businesses frequently expressed concern over the availability and accessibility of government authorities. These criticisms highlight the lack of opportunities at the local level for large cultural enterprises to become involved in the CCEA.

1.5. Structure of the Book

The remained of this book is organised into eight chapters. Chapter 1 has served to introduce the book's context and has outlined the research problem addressed. Chapter 2 explores the arguments made for using culture within the context of urban regeneration theory and practice. Chapter 3 establishes a conceptual framework to aid the understanding of South Korea's current situation and its history of urban regeneration. Chapter 4 examines the history of cultural policy and identifies how it has been integrated within urban regeneration processes and touches on practical, cultural examples which have been adopted in regeneration processes after the passing of the Special Act of Urban Regeneration in 2013. Chapter 5 introduces the case study city and the three targeted neighbourhoods that form the basis for the empirical investigation of the book; - Cheongju, Jungang-dong, Naedeok-dong and Suamgol, and scrutinises the CCEA in relation to the context, management and impacts of the event in Cheongju. In Chapter 6, the impact of CCEA, as shown through this research's questionnaire and interviews, is analysed. This chapter particularly focuses on the community development impacts of the CCEA. Finally, Chapter 7 offers an overview of what has been achieved in regard to the CCEA in 2015. Thereafter, the implications of this book for the management of cultural events and culture-led urban regeneration initiatives are discussed.

Chapter 2

What is Culture-led Urban Regeneration?

2.1. What is Urban Regeneration, and What Does It Seek to Do?

Cities are ceaselessly changing and facing repeated development and decline. In this process, multiple challenges, including physical deterioration, environmental issues, demolition and preservation, security, and economic and social inequalities, need to be tackled. In order to solve such challenges, cities introduce various approaches such as urban redevelopment and urban regeneration schemes. Different approaches are reflected in the targeted cities because all cities have their own situations and problems.

Prior to the 1970s, the dominant idea for developing cities was urban renewal through physical interventions or property-led development. Such initiatives focused upon large scale housing improvements, the bulldozing of deteriorated areas, and property development. The aim was to improve living conditions in a time of economic growth. However, many renewal initiatives de-emphasised community and society improvements by focusing primarily on the construction of new buildings and replacing undesirable land uses with high-density housing. Urban planning that focuses merely on the property-centred scheme is no longer the best option for changing declined urban environments. To tackle the drawback of renewal schemes, the term 'urban regeneration' has become a buzzword and an important sphere of public policy in many countries around the world over the last three decades. As the concept of urban regeneration appeared in the 1980s, it sought to ameliorate the negative consequences of deindustrialisation such as widespread depopulation, the decline of traditional industries, loss of employment opportunities, and dereliction within cities. The general underlying principles of regenerative projects are to improve the economic, social and physical circumstances of deprived and disadvantaged areas and households by adapting the existing built environment. More specifically, issues such as improving unemployment, crime reduction, education and health are important goals in all regeneration programmes and seek to minimise the disadvantages of derelict areas.

Furthermore, a distinctive characteristic of urban regeneration is that it encourages and seeks the fullest possible engagement and co-operation of multiple agencies, including the public, private and voluntary sectors. Enhancing equal partnerships between these sectors can build "shared interests, reciprocal support and mutual benefit with each partner contributing according to their respective resources, strengths and areas of expertise" (Carter, 2000, p.49). Such partnerships can bring dynamism to addressing the problems of urban renewal. In fact, the top-down approach that had generally been used in the process of urban renewal schemes. In this approach, it could not ensure the impartial representation of different interests of stakeholders, interact closely with local authority and residents, and be responsive to local needs because of its growth-centred aims. However, bottom-up strategies are able to generate more positive synergies and can provide effective solutions at a local level as local residents can be active participants. Bottom-up strategies in the process of urban regeneration give real power to communities and residents to make their own decisions about what kinds of infrastructure and planning they want for their communities.

Table 2-1. Meaning of urban regeneration explained by academic researchers

"Urban regeneration moves beyond the aims, aspirations and achievements of urban renewal, which is seen as a process of essentiality, physical change, urban development (or redevelopment) with its general mission and less well-defined purpose and urban revitalisation (or re-habitation) which whilst suggests the need for action fails to specify a precise method of approach" (Couch, 1990, p.2). Urban regeneration has sought to ameliorate economic, social environment transformation of derelict urban areas (Jones and Evans, 2008) "A comprehensive and integrated vision and action which leads to the resolution of urban problems, and it seeks to bring about a lasting improvement in the economic, physical, social and environmental conditions of an area that has been subject to change" (Roberts, 2000, p. 17)

As the pure purposes of urban regeneration are to ensure affordability, involve communities in programmes that deliver long-term sustainability, and protect locality and existing buildings, its effectiveness can be addressed in economic, social and environmental sectors. With regard to economic impacts, it is difficult to evaluate impact due to the unpredictability of each programme. Nevertheless, general impacts with regard to economic improvement include enhancing inward investment, boosting local employability, bringing creative businesses and people, encouraging horizontal co-operation between multiple-agencies (government, local authorities, institutes, academy and local residents), and increasing property value in residential and business areas. Such above impacts can lead to a long-lasting change in the local economy. With regard to the social sector, regenerative projects can deliver success when responding to local communities and residents. In this sense, urban regeneration largely contributes to enhancing community involvement as residents have empowerment over their lives, can contribute to programmes that promise to sustain the given community. Also, it may impact upon reducing crime and the improvement of security provision through providing appropriate schemes and facilities (e.g. neighbourhood watch, community centres, street lighting, neat management of targeted area such as fly-tipping and rubbish, and handling unattended places or houses). With regard to environmental or physical improvement, upgrading the landscaping and planting, improving accessibility to sites, creatively treating vacant or derelict spaces, developing a surrounding environment of industrial and residential areas, and preservation of locality and traditional building are all representative positive impacts of the urban regeneration scheme. Providing a deeper understanding of urban regeneration, this book focuses on culture and arts as an approach to deliver successful urban regeneration.

2.2 The Rise of Arts and Culture in Regeneration

In the context of urban regeneration, the terms culture and arts embrace a wide range of categories, from architecture and design to cultural activities, artistic works, and the cultural events (i.e. sports, festivals, expo, and so on.), as well as creativity and the knowledge economy (Jones and Evans, 2008). Before the 1960s, the meaning of culture was weighted so that almost all cultural components had a close relationship with 'high culture' without any recognition of economic impacts. Between the 1960s and the 1970s, however, the need to integrate culture with the economy was recognised within municipal authorities, and there was a post-materialist cultural shift to promote cultural elements in more effective ways. Since this time, many cities have started to recognise that culture can be a beneficial trigger to help make cities competitive and improve their economic circumstances. From the beginning of the 1990s onward, cultural materials began to attract attention as a way to create urban development, alongside a growth in interest in the benefits associated with the creative economy. Throsby (2010, p.2) expressed that as the term culture has enlarged its application to cultural policy, the scope of cultural policy has transformed from "a concern solely with the arts and heritage to a broader interpretation of culture as a way of life". Combining cultural and artistic productions and any type of public policy – from economic improvement to housing, city planning, social issues, and education – possesses synergistic correlations (Landry, 2003). It shows that cultural intervention is a powerful communication and culture-related policy which has become a crucial segment in urban planning. In addition, culture and arts play a significant role in creating new post-industrial urban identities. It has been recognised that culture and arts, and policies to promote culture, cannot exist in isolation and should instead be closely integrated with several realms to improve urban regeneration initiatives.

Over the last 30 years, there has been a growing interest in the possibilities for culture-led urban regeneration, often based around investment in large-scale cultural events or facilities. This burgeoning interest reflects the increased consumption of arts and culture in society, as well as the sector being increasingly recognised as a source of jobs and investment, as well as city re-imaging. For instance, art galleries or sports stadiums possess anchoring qualities for regeneration programmes, and such an obvious manifestation of flagship cultural institutions attracts private investment in declining areas. Furthermore, various cultural inputs such as local events, artwork exhibitions, festivals (e.g. expo, biennial, flea-markets, etc.), which promote traditional cultural assets and so forth are recognised as a way to bring employment and tourism to suburban areas which have suffered from industrial decline. Accordingly, a distinctive characteristic of integrating cultural elements within urban strategies including design, artworks, cultural activities and architecture – is indissoluble with not only people's lifestyle but also socio-economic prospects.

2.3. Positivity of Using Culture and Arts in Regeneration Scheme

There is no doubt that the development of arts and culture has emerged as a significant component of wider policies for regenerating post-industrial or declining cities. In order to prove the effects of the same, this section explores the positivity of cultural interventions within urban regeneration strategies. As a matter of fact, cultural activities, arts and sport can contribute to wider sectors that are considered imperative within urban regeneration - health, crime, employment, educational attainment, social cohesion, community development, and so on. It is believed that culture and arts have achieved prominence in being a force for economic development, physical (environmental) improvement and community development. In terms of physical regeneration, policies related with culture and arts can be used to promote the quality of the public realm, re-use redundant buildings, create environmental improvements, and increase the public use of space; all can lead to reductions in vandalism and increased senses of safety, pride in a place, changes of living and working circumstance, and the incorporation of cultural considerations into future plans. Furthermore, culture and arts can directly or indirectly influence economic sectors through inward investment, higher resident and visitor spending, job creation, the creation of a more diverse workforce, the development of new business, an increased number of public-private-voluntary sector partnerships (e.g. more corporate involvement in the local cultural sectors), and increased property prices in residential and business areas.

Apart from impacts within physical and economic sectors, culture and arts can be a primary tool of empowerment by which to achieve wider social regeneration; this book highlights the social impacts generated by using culture and arts on educational achievement, health, social inclusion, crime, and so on. For instance, arts, music classes, and performances can play a tacit role in enhancing an individual's literacy or social communication skills and breed community cohesion between residents of different ages and different cultural backgrounds - one of the most imperative purposes of urban regeneration. In addition, the cultural participation of residents can foster social improvement regarding personal growth, increase individual potential, and boost self-confidence as well as senses of self-worth. These individual factors can strengthen people's social networks, improve employability prospects, and provide a positive sense of identity for people at risk of exclusion such as disadvantaged people, disabled people and minority ethnic groups. As the ultimate purpose of urban regeneration is to bring lasting improvement to people's lives and improve the social conditions of the regeneration targeted area, cultural intervention is a good driver to achieve the aims. It is certainly believed that well-organised management, the cultural programmes encouraging community participation and community-led cultural inputs could bring social regeneration of an area that has been subject to improve. Its actual impacts are discussed in Chapter 6 with regard to a case study of South Korea.

Figure 2-1: Positive effects of cultural intervention on social regeneration

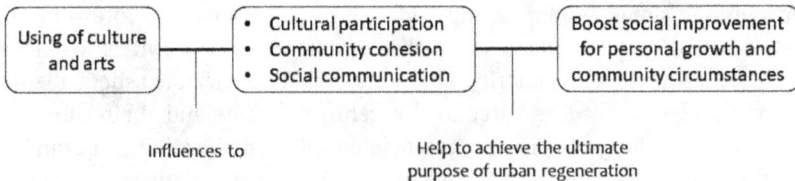

Author

2.4. Potential Tensions and Limitations in the Use of Arts and Culture to Support Regeneration

Undoubtedly, urban regeneration initiatives should ensure equal access to all areas including physical, environmental, economic and social spheres. Yet there is particular controversy over combining economic and social approaches to urban regeneration. As priorities have moved away from physical regeneration towards forms of social and economic regeneration, being able to balance economic and social effects has become key to urban regeneration efforts, especially as economic and social approaches can appear to have different objectives and purposes. For example, economic-led regeneration is largely focused on inner-city investment, consumer spending, attracting a skilled workforce and raising property values. On the other hand, social regeneration tries to tackle problems associated with unemployment, poverty and crime, while also trying to improve poor amenities, and improve both education and housing conditions. In many economic regeneration projects, central government and local authorities coordinate their efforts to boost economic growth within an area mainly using a property-led approach. Sometimes, these approaches consider a property-orientated project as key to creating benefits for local people and small business in poor neighbourhoods. However, such initiatives can cause problems and can often fail to address social and environmental problems. They may also fail to respond to local community needs and can often result in public money being used to subsidise private investors. Ginsburg (1999) emphasises that public buildings, leisure facilities, public transport, new apartments and employment opportunities are major elements of urban regeneration, but also notes how regeneration initiatives should not exclude the welfare and economic well-being of residents and small businesses, or the cohesion of communities in the targeted areas.

In the development of cultural approaches to urban regeneration, there have been diverse contentions. First, there is a dilemma with regard to cultural funding. Allocating an appropriate balance of investment in temporary and permanent cultural activities is complicated. Bianchini (1993) argues that reckless investment in landmark infrastructures might generate the creation of expensive, white-elephants and cause problems of gentrification in surrounding areas. Hallmark focused investment can often interrupt the development of local culture or small-sized community activities (e.g. local festivals, residents-led or charity-led events, etc.). In the spatial aspect, there is the challenge of needing cater to the centre of cities and their suburban surroundings, alongside problems associated with gentrification. For example, a number of mega-sized cultural events may offer a superlative geographical distribution of cultural programmes, including within the most deprived areas of a city, but many of them fail to establish sustainable structures to carry after the event has been completed. Sometimes, the cities that host cultural events such as the European Capital of Culture, the Olympics and the International Biennale provided to create a geographical balance in the aspect of equal cultural provision. However, such cultural investments aspire to refurbish unused or unattractive amenities through relocating high-income groups or creative people while placing pressure on low-income groups and often pushing them further to the margins (Garcia, 2004).

Another unsolved contradiction exists between economic and cultural priorities in regenerative initiatives. As many cities introduce culture and arts for inducing economic innovation and surviving in the increasingly competitive global era, the key questions still remain as to how such economically competitive cities can retain authentic local characteristics, and what is the value of cultural elements in the competitive global marketplace? The use of culture to sell places in the context of urban regeneration could actually spoil indigenous local cultures and identities by focusing on big-name commercial and private sponsors and the desire to attract large audiences. In this case, economic factors may be prioritised over providing a unique cultural strategy tailored to local characteristics. There are other prevalent controversies and tensions in the context of social regeneration, "culture is a means of spreading the benefits of prosperity to all citizens, through its capacity to engender social and human capital, improve life skills and transform the organisational capacity to handle and respond to change" (Comedia, 2003). Specifically, as cultural programmes are intervened in the regeneration targeted area, existing unskilled workers are often unable to access emerging employment in the new cultural sectors. Also, jobs generated by culture-led regeneration projects show usually unstable part-time, unreasonably low wages and low satisfaction.

There are still fundamental problems between these two aspects that have such as apparent incompatibility, generation disputes between the city centre and the suburbs, between private and public space, between existing residents and tourists, and between economic development and the improvement of quality of life. Indeed, cultural programmes cannot change the entire environment of deprived communities, and there are no straight forward answers. However, as many of culture-based projects present a slogan that tackles the social deprivation through injecting culture and arts, it should have a well-organised management process to address existing social problems occurring within the targeted areas.

With regards to the tensions that may exist between culture, arts and regeneration, but some lessons can be learned from previous culture-led initiatives. In order to maximise the impacts experienced within economic, social and cultural spheres Garcia (2004) argues that there are a series of key lessons: (a) capital investment and building schemes should be reliable and long-term cost planning, initiated at the beginning of the process, (b) to avoid the predominance of a top-down approach, the local community should be involved in the decision-making process, (c) cultural investment should promote the sustainable products of the local culture to encourage local consumption and sustainable exports, rather than infusing world-class products, (d) cultural investment in both people and the community's environment should be prioritised, (e) the achievements of culture-led regeneration is assessed through its cultural, economic and regenerative impacts in the long-term.

2.5. Actual Reflection from the Experience of Major Cultural Events

As discussed in Section 2.2, arts and culture can find their way into regeneration in different ways; small-scale activities or large-scale events, for example. Urban regeneration, specifically social regeneration, might be a benefit to wider cultural activities. As this book looks at a particular feature of arts and culture-regeneration, this section explores the experience of similar sorts of events that have already been held – the European Capital of Culture and the UK City of Culture (hereafter UKCOC).

The ECOC is a year-long cultural event and has been in operation since 1985. It highlights cultural diversity in Europe, encourages European citizens' sense of belonging to a common cultural area, and fosters the contribution of culture in regenerating cities. The event offers an opportunity to: invigorate cultural vibrancy and produce an image renaissance for a previously low-profile city; enhance local perception; increase cultural tourism; ensure active engagement of communities; and attract worldwide media attention. For the UKCOC, the inaugural competition was launched in the United Kingdom in July 2009. The motivation emerged from the successful ECOC experience of Liverpool in 2008 and sought to provide a symbolic handover to the Cultural Olympiad of 2012. Its fundamental vision was to put culture at the core of city agendas, policies and planning, and to use a cultural agenda as a decisive tool for social, civic, economic and participation agendas. Improving cultural sustainability through encouraging artistic strengths, social impacts, economic objectives, supporting existing organisations, as well as encouraging public-private partnerships, funding, enhancing tourism, refining governance arrangements and creating an after-event legacy were primary purposes. In order to identify its pieces of evidence, this section focuses on the ECOC (from Glasgow and Liverpool in the UK), and UKCOC (from London-Derry in Northern Ireland) events, that brings out the regenerative opportunities into the hosting cities.

- The 1990 ECOC in Glasgow

Glasgow's economy, based heavily on shipbuilding and metal manufacture, has dramatically declined since the 1970s, directly impacting urban deterioration and creating problems associated with severe violence and industrial unrest. In response to this, policymakers sought policies to invigorate the city's long-term physical and economic prospects. In order to host the ECOC, both the Glasgow District Council and the Strathclyde Regional Council drafted a list of specific objectives to enrich existing cultural organisation programmes, as well as mechanisms by which to pursue a more collaborative approach to cultural provision, and create employment opportunities as well as increase participation in cultural activities (Myerscough, 1991). In particular, the project organisers aimed to reach out to deprived communities, and promote social cohesion. In so doing, they launched a broad cultural remit that would impact on features such as religion, sport, and technology. Glasgow 1990 formed the foundations for how cultural events and the ECOC could regenerate the city, and kickstarted discussions on wider urban cultural policies.

Within the context of economic development, the Monitoring Glasgow Report 1990 by John Myerscough explains that the ECOC event brought a positive net economic return to the regional economy of £10.3 - 14.1 million. In addition, additional employment was calculated to be between 5,350 – 5,580; a number of sectors (e.g. business sponsorship, charitable trusts, corporate donations, and festivals office), other private giving including corporate memberships contributed to 340 to 350 new art businesses; and the commitment of the private sector to cultural events was valued at £6.1 million. According to the Scottish Tourist Board, between 1991 and 1998 UK tourists travelling to Glasgow rose by 88% while the foreign tourist rate between 1991 and 1997 grew by 25%, with a 200% increase in conference sales since 1997.

The 1990 ECOC also contributed to social aspects of urban life, impacting on education, the distribution of cultural benefits to marginal communities, the creation of a disability arts movement, and the creation of new social work programmes (Myerscough, 1991). The Strathclyde Regional Council spent £1.95million on 677 educational initiatives, including school projects, community education, and regional projects to provide broader cultural opportunities to students. In order to offer various opportunities to ordinary, disabled and disadvantaged residents, many social work programmes were arranged by Glasgow's established arts and culture companies (e.g. Scottish Opera, Scottish Ballet, and the Scottish Academy of Music & Drama) to meet the specific needs of individuals and communities. These projects focused on gaining and using skills through cultural programmes. Specifically, creative writing sessions led to word processing and publishing techniques, music programmes offered a form of communication for the profoundly handicapped, the visual arts helped people suffering from dementia, and movement therapy techniques supported children with severe obstacles in verbal communication.

- The 2008 ECOC in Liverpool

The ECOC in Liverpool 2008 offers compelling lessons in culture-led urban regeneration in the context of "integrating the cultural sector into the administrative and decision-making network for the city" (O'Brien, 2011, p.46). In order to make a success of the city's ECOC, there was an unprecedented collaboration between public and private sectors, individuals and organisations, cultural partners, and local artists; all who worked together towards one mutual goal (Garcia, n.d.). Furthermore, the partnerships involved organisations such as tourist companies, national agencies, housing agencies, local communities, voluntary groups, sporting clubs, transport companies, cultural education institutions, and representatives from the health service. These efforts attracted 9.7 million additional visits to Liverpool during the ECOC, with an economic impact of £753.8 million across Liverpool, Merseyside, and the North West region.

With regards to the social dimension, volunteers and local participants reported a range of social outcomes. For instance, t social interactions caused by cultural involvement, the chance to welcome outsiders to the city, and the satisfaction of promoting the city's culture and heritage. The 08 Volunteer programme attracted 971 active volunteers, 15% of whom were black or minority ethnic, and 6.1% were disabled. Through the programme, volunteering participants gained "the opportunity to reach out to others and make connections and friendships", "great satisfaction from the feeling that they were making a positive contribution to the rehabilitation of Liverpool", and "knowledge of Liverpool's history, heritage and cultural offer, and developed their confidence and the skills in dealing with members of the public" (Garcia, Melville, and Cox, 2010, p. 22). According to the Impacts 08 Neighbourhood directed by Beatriz Garcia and reported by Ruth Melville, there was an active engagement during the ECOC across the city: 66% of residents took part in at least one ECOC event, and 14% participants strongly agreed that they had done something new, including visiting a cultural space for the first time or attending a different type of event. Those who were involved in the cultural programmes appeared more likely to feel a positive relationship with their community.

- The 2013 UK City of Culture in Derry-Londonderry

Derry-Londonderry is the second largest urban centre in Northern Ireland. It was known to be a heavily militarised area with widespread civil unrest from the beginning of the 1970s until the time of the Good Friday Agreement. In 2009, the city was classified as the poorest area in Northern Ireland when compared with 25 other District Council areas. The city suffered from the worst level of economic deprivation in the province. To address the deficit in coherent regional physical development, in 1995, the City Vision Board recommended five main features of future policy: culture, economy, community development, community inclusion and environment. Particularly, Derry City Council said that "leisure and culture in its widest sense has a major impact on the quality of life in helping communities to come together in sharing a sense of identity" (Derry City Council website, n.d.). Furthermore, the city harnessed the importance of quality of life and economic improvements by exploring the capability of cultural elements, arts and leisure spheres as regeneration-delivering catalysts. This optimism became the catalyst for Londonderry winning the first-ever UKCOC in 2013.

To encourage a better quality of life for local residents and improve social aspects of urban life, there were several schemes associated with the UKCOC including "redeveloping the former Ebrington army barracks, the upgrade of the railway line and a multi-million-pound revamp of the public realm with around £80m investment" (Kivlehan, 2013). Bringing lasting improvement to the physical landscape of Derry enhanced the quality of life of local people. Furthermore, Derry particularly emphasised that "UKCOC is the focus on equality, good relations and social cohesion which are essential for transformation" (Derry City Council, 2009. p.31). The year-long event would boost civic identity, enable a wide range of cultural opportunities to be offered, and create active engagement of the public "within neighbourhoods by integrating cultural activities into the wider regeneration vision" (p.31). Shona McCarthy, the Chief Executive of Culture Company 2013, insisted that cultural programmes hosted at the schools, local communities and creative art sectors not only promoted creative practice, professional experience, and cultural participation but also remained the most prominent legacy of the UKCOC.

The UKCOC included high-art performances from the likes of the London Symphony Orchestra, the Royal Ballet, and the first staging of the Turner prize outside England. However, smaller and community events were also added to take culture on to the streets and make the programme accessible to as many people as possible (Graeme Farrow, the executive programmer, interviewed by Caines, 2015). For example, there were attempts to set world records for the longest River-dance, musical entertainment was held across various venues, and electronic music festivals also took place. Such events brought a sense of coming together in a city where wall murals still reflect historic sectarian divisions. Furthermore, UKCOC gained support from both unionist and nationalist communities, leading some to argue that united people in the city while creating opportunities for social interaction and tolerance. To encourage young people to take part, Derry provided new computers and creative teaching software for local schools and assembled a cast of young people to perform Hofesh Shechter's Political Mother production. Young participants said that they felt that they had become part of the event and owned what went on in their city. Thus, the cultural events affected not only inspires a new generation but also enabled diverse communities to cooperate and come together in supportive ways.

2.6. Limitations of Year-long Events

Apart from the positive impacts of the year-long events, the tensions between economic and social goals inherent within cultural approaches to regeneration have led to controversial issues within the events discussed in this chapter. In case of the Glasgow 1990, the event allowed the city to receive investment in capital projects of £43 million as well as investment in new or refurbished cultural facilities (e.g. Glasgow Concert Hall, McLellan Galleries, and Tramway). However, the systematic establishment of partnerships and workforce structures was neglected by event organisers who failed to form strategies that could allow further activities to be produced and distributed in subsequent years. As a result, the Glasgow ECOC was criticised for being eager to achieve economic benefits rather than ensuring that cultural legacies extended beyond 1990. Garcia (2004, p. 319) argued that "culture was used as an instrument for economic regeneration without being supported by a properly developed urban cultural policy". The economic-centred results by the Glasgow ECOC were listed by Mooney (2004), who stressed that it could result in more poverty, greater economic hardship and a growing divide between the 'haves' and the 'have nots' (p. 332).

One of the most common criticisms of Liverpool 2008 was the inappropriate geographical distribution of events. With regard to neighbourhood impacts, it was recorded that around half of the residents (56%) felt that only the city centre had benefited from ECOC in 2009. Also, 55% of respondents agreed that ECOC had made no difference to any neighbourhood. This rate of agreement was very high in certain communities, such as 84% in Kirkdale and 83% in Knotty Ash. On the other hand, 64% of respondents in the city centre felt that ECOC had made a difference in their neighbourhood. In conclusion, there was a lack of community engagement that was not facilitated from the bottom-up and through local structures, and the event was arguably hosted within safe areas.

As a means of strengthening the images of cities in the context of the global economy, improving the built environment, and encouraging social and tourism markets, a greater number of cities have been employing mega-cultural events recently. There is no doubt that a year-long cultural event like the ECOC and UKCOC can contribute to cultural vibrancy, produce an image renaissance for a previously low-profile city, and enhance local perceptions, whilst also increasing cultural tourism and attracting worldwide media attention. However, these mega-events still face challenges and dilemmas. These events have must also, however, to improve the environment of deprived communities, and address sustainable structure needs to maintain the balance between x and y once the events are over (Garcia, 2004). In terms of social impacts, it is important to utilise such mega-events to refurbish unused or unattractive amenities, although this may have the outcome of relocating high-income groups or creative people while placing additional pressures on low-income groups. Therefore, organisers should consider an appropriate balance of investment; between stimulating cultural consumption and supporting cultural production, whilst also ensuring that such events cater to both city centres and suburban areas. The dangers associated with gentrification also need to be avoided.

2.7. Summary

The potential benefits of adopting a cultural strategy for urban regeneration policies are many. Moreover, an adequate supply of cultural opportunities can generate sustainable benefits to individual communities as well as wider cities as a whole. However, as many cultural approaches to urban regeneration have been focused on the creation of flagship buildings or the hosting of mega-events, there are also concerns around the actual social impacts that such events have as well as their impacts on deprived communities. Jones and Evans (2008, p.138) stress that such events or symbolic cultural infrastructures "are only as successful as the uses to which they are put, and high-profile flops have left some areas with embarrassing and very expensive white elephants for which new uses have to be found". This might also lead to periodic economic or social deprivation in a particular area. Despite the complexities and contradictions of urban regeneration initiatives, it remains the case that the use of culture and arts is still a mainstream of urban regeneration policy and will play an ever more important role in future regeneration initiatives.

Chapter 3

Urban Regeneration History and Scheme in South Korea: Exploring the Context and Practice Applied in Urban Regeneration Initiatives

In South Korea, urban regeneration has gained a large public profile within the Korean urban policy agenda since the early 2000s and enjoys significant contemporary public interest. To fully understand the concepts discussed within this work, it is important, to begin with, an understanding of what the concept of 'urban regeneration' means in South Korea. The term urban regeneration does not have a strong history in South Korea, and there is only limited academic and policy literature on the topic. In this country, urban regeneration has not been a key concern as priority has instead been given to urban clearance and redevelopment projects; mainly to upgrade poor-quality housing, promote economic development and secure investor profit. However, social issues and the views of community groups, often ignored in previous processes of redevelopment, have now become more prominent in programmes that seek to deliver sustainable growth and development within urban areas in South Korea. In this sense, urban 'regeneration' has become a buzzword for rectifying the problems associated with redevelopment policies. Urban regeneration seeks to focus on social and community issues rather than purely upon economic and property benefits. It can be argued that policymakers within South Korea have recognised the importance of pursuing an urban regeneration policy that simultaneous combination of improving physical fabric, economic circumstances, social structures and environmental conditions.

3.1. The Impacts of Urbanisation and the Emergence of Urban Redevelopment Schemes in South Korea

To comprehend why the concept of urban regeneration has risen in importance in South Korea, it is first necessary to appreciate the process of urban redevelopment and its possible implications. As part of the modernisation efforts which followed the Korean War (1950 to 1953), South Korea experienced an unprecedented increase in urbanisation and industrialisation. Urbanisation rose dramatically from 35.8% to 85% between 1960 and 1995. During this period, South Korea developed from being a poor nation with an agricultural base and became a global industrial powerhouse. For instance, Seoul's population swelled from 2.5 million in 1962 to 10 million in 1988 through rural-urban migration and people returning from abroad, after having fled abroad due to Japanese occupation and the Korean War. Busan (one of the metropolitan cities of South Korea) experienced radical urbanisation from 37% in 1960 to 87.8% in 2000. Furthermore, the urbanisation rate has continued to grow; 89.87% in 2004 to 91.66% in 2014 according to the average rate of main capital cities (e.g. Seoul, Busan, Daegu, Gwangju, Incheon and Daejeon). 47 million people currently live in cities, out of a total population of 51 million (Ministry of Land, Infrastructure and Transport (hereafter, MOLIT, 2015a).

Figure 3-1: Declining cities in South Korea

Declining Cities in **South Korea**

Urban Decay begins .... 41 areas

Urban Decay in Process .... 55 areas

overall 96 areas

SEOUL

DAEGU

BUSAN

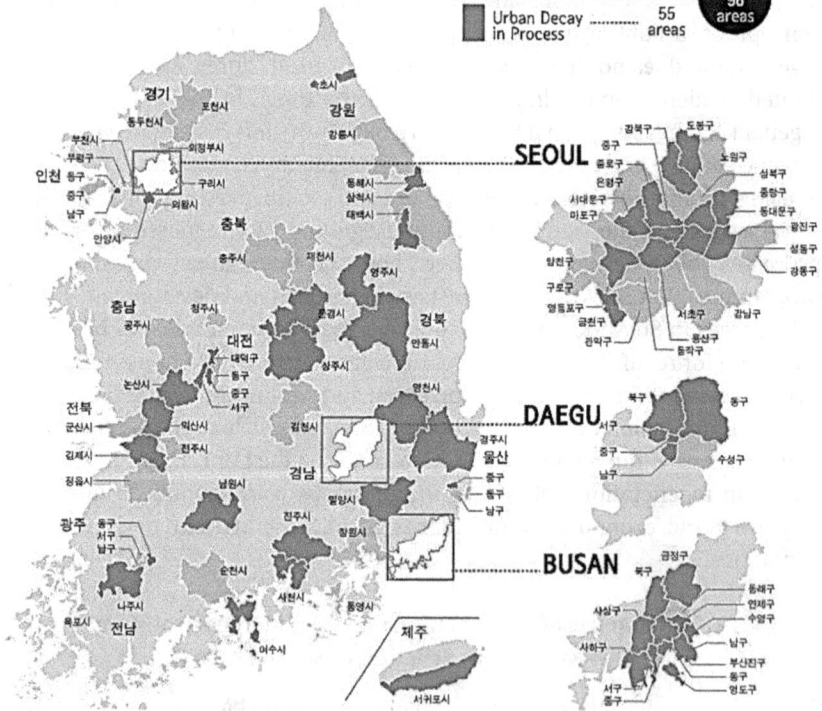

Source: MOLIT and KURC (2013). p.6

This rapid urbanisation triggered inevitable changes to the socio-economic environment, led to a lack of developable land, a persistent housing shortage, and the growth of squatter settlements. In many capital cities, there is, as a result of such processes, urban deprivation including social polarisation, economic hardship, residential environment degradation, traffic congestion, over-rapid growth and overpopulation. The concentration of people, buildings and economic activities in major cities has arguably resulted in low quality infrastructure and living environments. In this regard, as shown in Figure 3-1, between 2005 and 2010, there has been a significant increase in the concentration of deprivation, with 96 inner-city areas having high-level concentrations of deprivation out of 114 areas in South Korea (MOLIT and Korea Urban Regeneration Centre, hereafter, KURC).

To solve the various urban problems which have arisen from urbanisation, a number of urban remedies have been trialled since the 1960s. A key issue is the dominance of physical redevelopment from the 1960s onwards based on the removal of slum dwellings and the efficient utilisation of urban land in support of economic development.

3.2. Brief Explanation Regarding with Urban Redevelopment of South Korea

The brutal consequences of the Korean War left many cities in South Korea ravaged in 1953. From the 1960s onwards, the priority of urban development was to remove poor quality infrastructure and slum-dwelling in cities. To achieve this, office blocks were newly built on land where previously slums had existed, and traditional homes and historic buildings were replaced by numerous blocks of flats through ambitious state-led programs. This post-Korean War urban redevelopment strategy drew a massive wave of rural migrants and refugees from outlying areas into the capital cities. This was reinforced with the industrialisation of the 1960s and 1970s, and the massive influx of people from suburban and rural areas meant that cities experienced an acute housing shortage. This problem was, in turn, further accentuated by the inadequate provision of fundamental infrastructure, and the weak environmental quality that average citizens experienced. The lack of housing caused a rise in squatter settlements in the surrounding mountains and hillsides of cities. To tackle the problems and accommodate more labour, the government launched an urban redevelopment project called New Town. This programme sought to relocate squatter settlements from the central urban areas to the surrounding suburbs and had two primary overarching goals; to provide resolution to urban problems in large cities, and to stabilize the national territory.

Table 3-1. Large-scale eviction project of New Town]

After 1966 a sequence of large-scale eviction projects was undertaken. The Seoul central government undertook its first major slum clearance project; planned replacement of 136,000 squatter units with 90,000 public housings in Gwangju (recently called Seongnam). Central government bulldozed through mountains and built over rivers to build roads, state-sponsored mass housing and new urban infrastructures. However, during this period, people living in squatter settlements were often forcibly removed by the state without proper provision for their resettlement. This led to the displacement of more than 230,000 people. The initial aim of the project was to clear 130,000 poor housing units within three years and re-build 90,000 public housing units to provide living accommodation for those who had been displaced. More than 70,000 housing units were destroyed, with only 16,000 housing units being reconstructed by 1970. Only a small number of residents benefitted from higher standards of housing than those which that they had hitherto enjoyed. It also led to the displacement of a majority of slum residents and forced them into suburban areas near forests, national parks, and rivers, usually on government-owned land without sufficient infrastructure.

In the 1970s, the New Town policy as a redevelopment strategy became more pronounced, especially after the passing of the Urban Redevelopment Act (hereafter URA) in 1976. Aside from Seoul, several other municipal governments also embarked on slum clearances after the passing of the URA. A development-centred approach was designed to boost the national economy, and land was mobilised as a production element to encourage economic growth. However, this state-led urban redevelopment approach focused heavily on physical intervention and failed to tackle the gap between economic and social inequalities created by structural economic and social changes. Many of the benefits that arose from the redevelopment strategies went to private developers (e.g. private construction companies) and the state (which could benefit from selling off government-owned land and collecting more tax). There was little benefit to existing residents.

The 1980s heralded change. . As the country became more industrialised and transformed into a high-technology society, the traditional urban fabric and quality of existing buildings dramatically changed. Traditional buildings were replaced by high-rise complexes and skyscraper apartments. The Seoul Redevelopment Planning Report published by the Seoul Institute in 2001 highlights that whilst the demands for development were relatively patchy during the 1970s, during the 1980s the active implementation of the redevelopment strategy began in earnest with the rapid growth of mega-sized firms, an increased tertiary industry in urban areas, and the hosting of mega-sports events such as the 1986 Asian Games and the 1988 Olympics. The widespread development of skyscrapers and luxurious buildings changed the image and appearance of South Korea's cities.

Table 3-2. Forcible urban redevelopment project in Seoul for the 1988 Olympics

The International Olympic Committee (IOC) announced that South Korea would host the 1988 Summer Olympic Games in 1981. This sparked interest in urban regeneration projects, and the Olympics brought heightened demand for land to build sports venues, tourist facilities and accommodation for athletes and visitors. Such construction led to the significant spatial pattern of evictions. In 1983, the Korean government listed 227 areas for renewal by 1990, and during the five-year Olympic preparation period 48,000 buildings, housing units and 720,000 people were evicted without any replacement housing being in place. As a result, the redevelopment projects made significant numbers of people homeless, with widespread evictions (Greene, 2003). This forcible eviction programme in Seoul is still considered to have been the largest government-sponsored eviction programme to have taken place globally over the past few decades (Scott, 1995).

Furthermore, the 1980s was the period when the partnership started between Chaebol (A large family-owned business conglomerate in South Korea) and private construction companies. Bringing Chaebol into the projects was considered as crucial to fast-tracking South Korea's economic development, and the urban redevelopment plans were solely managed by the state and the large conglomerates. The large companies and construction firms began to make substantial profits through development schemes such as the construction of high-rise apartments in poor quality housing areas. For example, the New Town projects were expanded to tackle the problems of six capital cities (Seoul, Busan, Daegu, Gwangju, Incheon and Daejeon). In the case of Seoul, five new towns (Bundang, Ilsan, Pyeongchon, Sanbon and Joondong) were created in the late 1980s to alleviate overcrowding, the shortage of housing supply, and tackle housing price inflation within 20 kilometres of the city. However, the New Town policy largely overlooked social and economic factors and triggered socio-economic polarisation. Such intervention brought coercive evictions, and the New Town programmes also failed to create partnerships between property owners and developers. Tenants were forced to leave redevelopment sites and received only poor guarantees of relocation.

The period between 2002 and 2006 was considered as a boom period for the New Town redevelopment initiative under the direction of the former Mayor of

Seoul, Lee Myung-bak (also former president of South Korea from 2008 to 2013, and a housebuilder before becoming mayor). Mayor Lee enthusiastically advocated the New Town project to balance house prices and alleviate economic inequality. Concurrently, the Urban and Residential Environment Improvement Act (hereafter UREIA) was passed in 2002 which contained various types of redevelopment elements such as the Residential Improvement Project; Housing Redevelopment; Housing Reconstruction Project and the Urban Environmental Redevelopment Project. The UREIA initially led to the acceleration of urban redevelopment projects. The principle aims of these were to remedy the deteriorating residential environment by combining urban strategies and the necessary laws. In addition, the Act integrated and consolidated several previous laws – the Housing Construction Promotion Act (1972), the Urban Redevelopment Act (1976) and the Temporary Measures for Residential Improvement of Urban Low-income Group (from 1989 to 2004) (Legislation, 2011). The main aims of the UREIA were to ameliorate the redevelopment problems which had arisen from previous attempts such as the dwelling instability of tenant, eviction of residents and unreasonable increases in housing and 'jeonse'[1]. However, reconstructing a derelict area, bulldozing slum areas, and building sky-scraper apartments for profit have been still bringing negative results in the targeted local areas (Lim, 2013).

Another problem was that the UREIA placed the protection of the private ownership of domestic property as its first priority, thereby pushing the needs of residents to one side. Land-owner associations were created to maximise property values in targeted areas, and they took responsibility for signing contracts with private development companies (Kyung and Kim, 2011). As a result, a tenant or merchant without property had no input into the processes. The Act's main aim – to foster a better living environment for low-income residents – was largely ignored.

Table 3-3. The UREIA project in Cheongju

As the UREIA was implemented in Cheongju, it designated 39 districts of Cheongju (with 2,870,113m²) as UREIA targeted areas. The size of the project surpassed the new-town project at that time. The purpose of the UREIA was to increase the number of households from 17,630 to 63,810 households and to expand the population from 48,620 to 178,778. In undertaking these

---

[1] Jeonse: South Korea's unusual rental system, known as jeonse, does not involve monthly rental payments. Instead, tenants provide landlords with a deposit, typically between a quarter and half of the property's value, to invest for the duration of the lease. Property owners keep the returns and then repay the lump sum at the end of the tenancy.

mega-sized redevelopment projects, the local authority signed contracts private developers and investors, who provided the capital financing and subsequently managed the project. However, when oil prices reached record highs, and the global economic crisis began in 2008, tensions between public, private and residents began to escalate due to the growing financial difficulties experienced by the construction firms. The biggest issue was the housing, as many had already been demolished in anticipation of redevelopment projects. Members of the public, private developers and investors blamed each other for the crisis, and there were constant delays in remedial actions which caused social polarisation, social exclusion, community breakdown and economic loss.

Another serious problem was that there was no lead construction company in charge of overseeing the project due to the real-estate downturn. Therefore, recruiting appropriate developers became difficult and led to indefinite project delays. It could be argued that the failure of the initiatives and the problems emerging within surrounding environments emerged as a result of such an ambitious planning scheme being launched by a city authority which lacked sufficient management capacity.

During the same period, another serious dispute emerged between private companies and residents. Local residents wanted to maintain the local economic structure and its associated features, however, private developers were more concerned with maximising profits and restructuring the local economy. A number of private companies engaged in undemocratic actions, for example, one outsourced engineering company violently threatened residents who strongly opposed the redevelopment initiative. Thus, a democratic deficit emerged, which evidence a lack of trust between residents and developers. During the UREIA procedure, there was not enough explanation in relation to the project, so some of the low-income residents faced eviction by private developers without appropriate compensation scheme. It seemed that the initiative focused on achieving private benefits. In practice, the community needed more investment in basic infrastructure such as warehousing or cultural facilities rather than the building of high-rise apartments or lavish towers. However, the government and private companies were indifferent to residents' opinions and needs.

To tackle these problems, the central government and Cheongju Council amended the UREIA in 2012 so that private companies and the redevelopment committee could be dismissed by residents' agreement. This policy aimed to strengthen residents' empowerment in enhancing the districts in which they lived. As a result, the designated redevelopment districts were reduced from 39 to 24 by 2014. Amongst 24 districts, only one was successfully embarked on the project, while other districts demonstrated slow progress.

Due to the collapse of the urban redevelopment initiative, Cheongju has attempted to provide a more practical and holistic strategy to local residents since 2014. As an alternative strategy, urban regeneration became an attempt to prevent rapid deterioration, crime growth, social exclusion, and community malfunction, which all were caused by urban redevelopment scheme. As an urban regeneration strategy, regenerating the above 24 revocation areas became a high priority to be tackled through cooperative works between the public, private and local community partnerships.

With the development approach discussed above being increasingly criticised and problematic, the term 'urban regeneration' emerged as an alternative approach from the late 2000s onwards. The construction of modern apartments has still proliferated in South Korea, but urban regeneration schemes have become a potent alternative by which to revitalise deprived areas; especially within a large number of cancelled New Town sites. Urban redevelopment is a crucial issue in South Korea by which to reinforce the housing environment. However, it can frequently cause not only environmental or physical problems but also social problems, including the collapse of social networks and community destruction. In this regard, the practical intervention of urban regeneration has become an indispensable way to secure and protect inner-city areas and communities. The following section explores the importance of urban regeneration strategies in South Korea and examines how they intended to reduce social problems arising from previous schemes, and give rise to the emergence of solid legislation to support regeneration plans.

3.3. Urban Regeneration in South Korea

Urban regeneration, as a concept, emerged in South Korea around 2000 and has a different emphasis to urban redevelopment. A number of practical and academic experts have argued that urban regeneration offers an opportunity to rectify the mistakes made through previous urban renewal and new town projects (Song, 2010, Kang, 2014, and Yoon and Nam, 2015). As examined above, urban redevelopment projects offered an opportunity to eradicate the physical problems that arose following the Korean War; however, in many ways, the priorities of slum clearance, the new towns, and the processes of reconstruction led to other problems arising such as poor area designations, urban sprawl, property-led construction, biased benefits for private investors rather than existing residents, community breakup and social exclusion. To tackle these problems efficiently, specific urban regeneration policy was established in 2013. This section deals with the structures of urban regeneration policy and practical approaches to urban regeneration in detail.

- Before the Legislation of Urban Regeneration Policy: Practical Action for Local Development from the 1960s to 2000s

Although the term urban regeneration has recently emerged as an alternative procedure to urban redevelopment scheme, there have been the precedent regenerative attempts for local development in South Korea. The first practical participatory action for local development was called 'Saemaul Undong '(hereafter, SU), which was created by former President Park Chung-hee to modernise the rural economy of South Korea in 1970. The SU was also called the 'New Village Movement' and was a community-driven development built on the basis of institutional principles (e.g. diligence, self-help, and cooperation as the guiding operational principles) and community participation (Asian Development Bank, 2012). The principal aim of the SU movement was to provide individual and community well-being through poverty reduction, the improvement of fundamental infrastructure, enhanced public services, the empowerment of local communities, the revitalisation of community environments, and fostering the acceptance of women in social participation (many Asian societies have rigid and traditional gender-biased roles). Perhaps even more important to the long-term sustainability of South Korea was the aim of the SU to stimulate people's mentality. The SU movement "built a national confidence infused with a can-do spirit that transformed the former national mind-set of chronic defeatism into new hope, a shared vision of a better life for all, and an infectious enthusiasm propelled by volunteerism at the community level" (Asian Development Bank, p. 2). As a result, the movement positively impacted on household income growth, revolutionised the lives of rural villagers, improved social capital, fostered the empowerment of communities through self-help and self-reliance, and offered gender liberation through encouraging women to engage politically. However, one big limitation of the SU was its top-down, centralised, command-and-control structure that governed local administration. These administrative policies frequently discouraged citizens from participating and often prevented new ideas from being incorporated into SU activities.

After the success of the SU, other community movements were created, such as the 'Urban Lower Class Movement' in the 1970s which sought to reduce poverty, the 'Opposition Movement against Urban Renewal' in the 1980s, and the 'Neighbourhood Recovery Movement' of the 1990s which sought to contribute to local development. There were also similar groups at the metropolitan level created by local authorities. As a representative example, the 'Raise the Best Village Project' (hereafter, RBVP) was created by the local authority of Jinan-gun in the North of Jeonla Province for developing rural areas in 2001. The strategies for this project were similar to the SU and the project adopted a primarily bottom-up approach, with an independent budget allocated for community development, a Task Force Team to pursue individual policies, and a budget for resident education offering sustainable community improvement (Haenam newspaper, 2006; Jin, Ryu, Jo, Kim, Kwon and Jung, 2007). The RBVP has continued since 2001 and regenerated more than 300 villages before 2010. The key to the success of RBVP was its ability to respect the opinions of ordinary residents with its main goals being to attract new businesses, integrate various professionals, and harmonise relationships with residents. The project is still referenced as a good example of community participation, and it has been influential in forming current urban regeneration policies in South Korea. The project also proved that derelict communities could be revitalised at the local government level, without entirely relying on central government finance or support.

The above resident-led actions and co-operative partnership between governments, private companies and citizen organisations have fostered the direction of urban policy and have created several 'Liveable Community Projects' (hereafter, LCPs), which were initiated at the end of the 1990s. The LCPs were officially institutionalised by the central government in 2005 (as they had similar key characteristics to existent urban regeneration policies) and the groups further encouraged resident participation. The LCPs was launched as the national urban policy by the Presidential Committee on Regional Development under the Special Act on Balanced National Development during the Noh Mu-hyun government (2004 to 2008). As part of government-wide efforts to enhance local environments, the project was jointly implemented by four different Ministries (Figure 3-2). Broadly similar policies applied in each project, although these were filtered through different Ministry structures within the framework of the LCP. The principle purpose of the LCP was to tackle nine fundamental needs of communities with regard to dwellings, welfare, work, environment, health, safety, culture, landscape and transportation spheres (Prism, 2009). As a bottom-up approach to development, the project also aimed to incorporate local residents into the decision-making processes, while additional government support (e.g. budget and administration supports) was allocated for stronger delivery arrangements.

Figure 3-2: The responsible ministries for the LCP

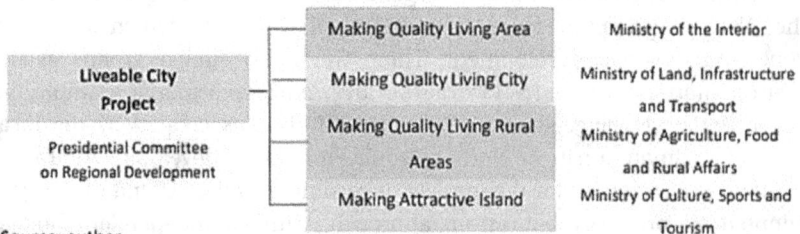

Liveable City Project Presidential Committee on Regional Development	Making Quality Living Area	Ministry of the Interior
	Making Quality Living City	Ministry of Land, Infrastructure and Transport
	Making Quality Living Rural Areas	Ministry of Agriculture, Food and Rural Affairs
	Making Attractive Island	Ministry of Culture, Sports and Tourism

Source: author

There have been various practical and specific projects undertaken within the LCPs, including the creation of a theme park around a railway, a traditional Korean village 'Hanok', a well-being theme park around a reservoir, more than 40 small parks, local food shops, and regular local festivals. However, the LCPs have noted that the policies pursued were generally limited to creating public-private partnerships, despite one main aim being to co-ordinate governance between the various sectors. The trust, reciprocity and capacity for resident engagement are considered to be essential elements in planning community-building events (Roberts, 2000). However, the LCPs often resulted in uneven trust-building between residents, leading organisations and Ministries. It has been argued that the policy-making period for the LCPs was too short and that this led to problems with regards to sustainability as well as unrealistic aims and objectives being embedded into policy.

In 2008, the central government administration changed from Noh Muhyun of the Democratic Party to Lee Myung-bak of the Conservative Party. The new government undertook a major review of urban policy in 2008, and in 2010 the LCP was expanded and became the 'City Vitality Promotion' (hereafter CVP). The new Act sought to improve four key areas: city vitality, general agricultural, mountain and fishing villages (which were allocated as regions needing fundamental infrastructure) and growth promotion. The initial purposes of the CVP were to improve living conditions in run-down areas, enhance the maintenance and construction of fundamental infrastructure, and to foster local programmes for community inclusion. From 2013, the Ministry of Land, Infrastructure and Transport (hereafter, MOLIT) designated 99 administrative units as CVP areas, which were then each targeted for one of four specific small-scale projects; 'residential regeneration', 'central area regeneration', 'expansion of basic living infrastructure' or 'strengthening local capacity'. In 2014, there were 155 CVP projects in 64 local government areas, including 26 residential regeneration projects, 58 central area regeneration projects, 54 expansion of basic living infrastructure projects, and 17 strengthening local capacity projects (MOLIT, 2015). In terms of finance, in 2016, the budget allocated to the CVP was integrated with the newly established urban regeneration scheme 67 to avoid overlapping financial support, as the two initiatives strived to achieve similar goals. The budget for both schemes was expanded from $40bn in 2015 to $144bn in 2016.

The trend towards urban regeneration has, therefore, been linked to changing modes of political action and urban governance. Different governmental departments have been involved, and different governance arrangements have been implemented, from SU in the 1970s to the CVP of today. Although the name or slogan of each project was different, and initiatives operated under different Acts and trialled different policies, these local development initiatives have become key in formulating current urban regeneration structures and arrangements. As the concept of urban regeneration has often been used ambiguously and covered various programmes of urban redevelopment, new town developments, and sometimes community programmes or local development projects, (Kim, 2010), the conceptual scope and cognition of urban regeneration has been abstractedly broadened. Over the years, there has been a lot of confusion relating to what is meant by urban regeneration at central and local levels. By recognising urban regeneration's growing importance, central and local governments, and many academics stress that the vague direction of urban regeneration schemes should have a legal basis in order to be effectively fulfilled (Gill, 2011 and Yu, 2013). In 2013, the central government of the Conservative party attempted to define the confused meaning and regulations of urban regeneration, using law terminology through establishing the Special Act on Urban Regeneration (hereafter SAUR) on 4th June 2013 (Seo and Yoon, 2015).

- Key Elements of the SAUR, South Korea from 2013 onwards

    I.   Urban regeneration policies in South Korea have had a range of impacts on the urban landscape, community revitalisation, changing the country's image, and socio-economic development. The Special Act on Urban Regeneration officially set out the shape of urban regeneration policy. Namely that

    II.   The central government supports local government and communities in formulating urban regeneration planning, and that this should include strategic and revitalisation planning. The main functional accountability of central government depends on the area's particular problems and potential.

    III.   It focuses not only on physical improvement but also on economic, social and environmental issues created under the old town regeneration strategies

    IV.   It makes decisions and supports communities through en-bloc deliberation of the urban regeneration select committee chaired by the Prime Minister

    V.   It provides package support (such as financial backing and administration support) special regulations, tax reductions, and tax exemptions including corporate tax, income tax, acquisition tax, registration and license tax and property tax (The SAUR article 2)

Under the SAUR, urban regeneration projects were restricted to being implemented in specific targeted areas, with several accepted types of urban regeneration initiatives listed in Article 2-7:

I.   A series of projects for local development and urban regeneration at a national level

II. A series of projects for local development and urban regeneration at the local government level

III. A community activation project by using the physical, social, human resources of local areas according to the local residents' suggestions

IV. A maintenance project according to the [Act on the maintenance and improvement of urban areas and dwelling conditions for residents], and renewal project by the [Special Act on the Promotion of Urban Renewal]

V.   An urban redevelopment project by the [Urban Redevelopment Act], and railway station improvement by the [Railroad Construction Act]

VI. Industrial complex development and regeneration projects by the [Industrial Sites and Development Act]

VII. Harbour redevelopment project by the [Harbour Act]

VIII. Commercial market activation project and traditional market area maintenance project by the [Special Act for promoting a traditional market and shopping district]

IX. Urban or district planning facility project by the [National Land Planning and Utilization Act], and a project by designating demonstration area

X.   A landscape project by the [Landscape Act]

XI. Any project which is necessary for enhancing urban regeneration by the presidential decree

The SAUR placed a greater emphasis on tackling complex socio-economic-environmental problems and revitalising local communities through collaboration between public, private, community and voluntary sectors (Seo and Yoon, 2015). Thus, the Act calls for greater coordination between local government, multi-agency and community groups (SAUR Article 3, 15 and 18). If local authorities wish to apply regeneration projects to their cities, they need to demonstrate a willingness and ability to affiliate and integrate with various governmental departments covering culture and tourism, welfare, economy, industry, land, infrastructure and transport (Article 9). To promote co-operation, central government provides direct guidance, including strategic planning for local or community levels, while an urban regeneration committee acts as a support system for joint action. Governmental departments (such as culture and tourism, welfare, agriculture, land and infrastructure) underpin urban regeneration projects in local communities.

- Specific Structure of Urban Regeneration Scheme since 2013: The Case of Cheongju

After the SAUR was implemented, the scale and intensity of the regeneration projects enacted at regional and local levels required the creation of a specialised agency for urban regeneration, called the National Urban Regeneration Intermediary Organisations (hereafter, NURIOs) to create sophisticated strategies and pump prime private investment into areas (Seo, Park and Lim, 2014). The NURIOs play a crucial role in linking the government's policy and delivery arrangements and guarantee direct funding from central government. According to this requirement, intermediary agencies (e.g. Urban Regeneration Centres, hereafter URC) were set up in many cities to deliver equitable and efficient solutions to locally owned problems. The URCs have no authority or powers over planning or land acquisition but are considered as coordinating bodies that can kick start investment within areas of deprivation. The URCs can be classified into four distinct categories in terms of management and administration: local government-led; public or local firm-led; local government and residents-led; and private-led commissioned by the local government. In the case of Cheongju's URC, the centre has established a partnership with Chungbuk University (commissioned by Cheongju city council) with five overarching ambitions:

I.   Economic regeneration: Use vacant or underused spaces such as shops, and establish areas for culture, leisure and entertainment use.

II.   Creation of Cheongju's regeneration: Share new terms and ideas, and develop a governance system for effective delivery.

III.   Creative regeneration: Excavate and discover valuable local assets, and pursue a wide range of culture-led regeneration.

IV.   Integrated regeneration: Maximise partnerships between central government, local authorities, other stakeholders and service providers for more integrated service provision and targeting the needs of deprived areas,

V.   Linked regeneration: Develop various regeneration programmes for a more secure, competitive and sustainable local future (Cheongju URC official website, n.d.).

Furthermore, to enhance an integrated approach and the formation of partnerships, the centre has attempted to create vertical and horizontal co-ordination with other local authorities since 2015 (e.g. Formed a partnership with Jecheon and Chungju in North Chungcheong Province). Such co-operative urban strategies are different compared to previous urban redevelopment strategies. With regard to the general managerial performance of the URC of Cheongju, it supports community-based business, discovers local assets, fosters community cohesiveness, actively works with existing communities, provides educational programmes about urban regeneration, assists social enterprises, and establishes partnerships between local authorities, key stakeholders and other delivery agencies.

- Approaches to Urban Regeneration: Economic-led, Social-led and Neighbourhood-led Regeneration

Under the SAUR, there are three overarching themes that aim to stabilise urban regeneration structures. They include economic-led regeneration, social-led regeneration at central and community levels, and neighbourhood-led regeneration (known as the Saddlemaeul project). In 2014, 13 of the most run-down areas were selected as the sites for inaugural urban regeneration projects (2 economic-led regeneration projects and 11 social-led regeneration projects. See Figure 3-3).

Figure 3-3: Thirteen pioneering areas of urban regeneration in 2014

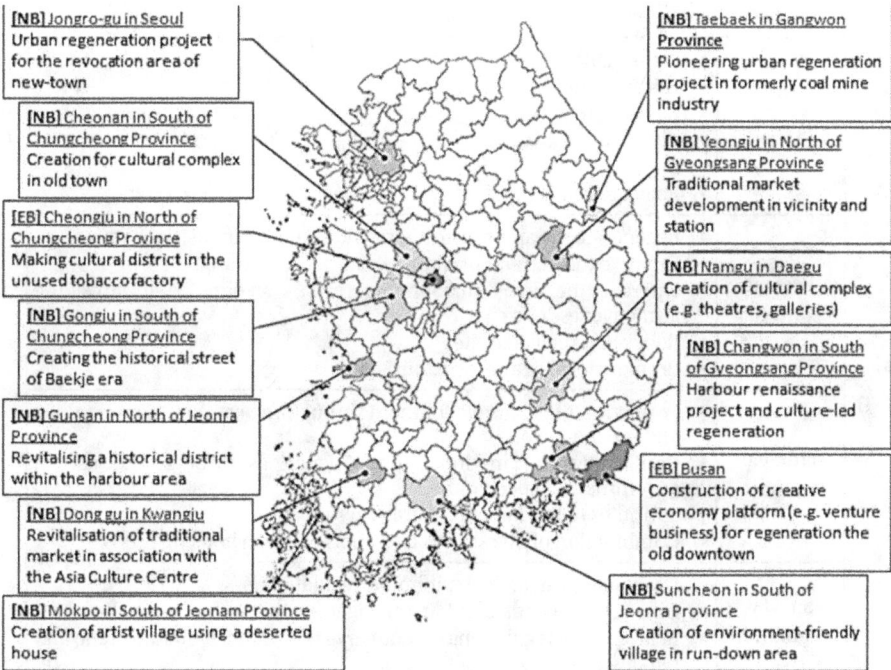

[NB] Jongro-gu in Seoul
Urban regeneration project for the revocation area of new-town

[NB] Cheonan in South of Chungcheong Province
Creation for cultural complex in old town

[EB] Cheongju in North of Chungcheong Province
Making cultural district in the unused tobacco factory

[NB] Gongju in South of Chungcheong Province
Creating the historical street of Baekje era

[NB] Gunsan in North of Jeonra Province
Revitalising a historical district within the harbour area

[NB] Dong-gu in Kwangju
Revitalisation of traditional market in association with the Asia Culture Centre

[NB] Mokpo in South of Jeonam Province
Creation of artist village using a deserted house

[NB] Taebaek in Gangwon Province
Pioneering urban regeneration project in formerly coal mine industry

[NB] Yeongju in North of Gyeongsang Province
Traditional market development in vicinity and station

[NB] Namgu in Daegu
Creation of cultural complex (e.g. theatres, galleries)

[NB] Changwon in South of Gyeongsang Province
Harbour renaissance project and culture-led regeneration

[EB] Busan
Construction of creative economy platform (e.g. venture business) for regeneration the old downtown

[NB] Suncheon in South of Jeonra Province
Creation of environment-friendly village in run-down area

Source: MOLIT website [Translated by author]
*EB stands for Economic-based regeneration / NB stands for Neighbourhood-based regeneration

I. Economic-led Urban Regeneration

Economic-led regeneration initiatives are characterised by a joint development on a former industrial area, harbour or railway station. In order to kick-start the economic-led urban regeneration project, the target area should demonstrate attractive investment opportunities and must be able to achieve investment and economic profitability. It is also important for selected areas to have untapped economic potential, such as core facilities that could provide economic renewal or sites that would create employment through repair and development. A structure of economic-led urban regeneration is noted in Table 3-4.

Table 3-4. Structure of Economic-led regeneration

ECONOMIC-LED REGENERATION	
Purposes	• Introduce new economic opportunities • Create employment opportunity through the conversion of existing industrial function and business • Spread economic recovery effect to an adjacent area
Target areas	• Unused industrial complexes • Harbour sites • Railway stations • Riverside • Airports • Relocated sites
Project contents	• Regenerate the areas surrounding now derelict industrial complexes • Improve the harbour or hinterlands' peripheral area • Upgrade the areas surrounding railway stations to improve the attractiveness of a city • Redevelop relocated sites • Promote local culture and tourism
Finance support	• Formation of economic foothold through the co-operation of public and private sectors • Contribution of in-kind support (such as through the use of government-owned land) • Subsidies to fundamental infrastructure • Combination of investment and loans of urban housing funds
Special regulation	• Designate as an area of minimum regulation • Change the agenda of urban management plan • Relaxation of regulations for floor area ratio, land to building ratio and parking standards
Inaugural leading areas	• Busan (Busan railway station ~ Busan harbour) • Cheongju (Surrounding 1.36km^2 area of formerly a tobacco factory in Naedeok 2 dong) *These two areas were selected in 2014 [Cheonan (19,865m^2 Land of Dongnam borough office), Bucheon (Wonmi gu), Daegu (Seogu) were chosen as an economic-led regeneration target areas in 2016]

Source: Kim (2015a), and MOLIT website (n.d.). [Translated by author]

Economic-led regeneration target areas also include former schools, military bases, and public offices. This approach is associated with a series of specific laws such as the Industrial Sites and Development Act, the Harbour Act, and the Railroad Construction and Safety Act, and so on). Table 3-5 outlines the outcomes expected through implementing an economic approach, the current difficulties experienced in targeted spaces, and the associated laws.

Table 3-5. The types of Economic-led urban regeneration

Types	Current Circumstances	Expected Outcomes	Related Law
Industrial Complex	• Equipment industry / low-value manufacturing industry-centred • Shortage of fundamental Infrastructure • Ineffective land use	• Location of high-tech manufacturing and integration industries • Attractiveness of multi-function areas such as culture, central business districts and dwellings	• Industrial Sites and Development Act
Harbour	• Struggling with decreasing harbour function • Ignorance of inner-harbour and dredged soil ground	• Creation of culture and tourism type harbour • Attractiveness of multi-function areas such as culture, central business districts and dwellings	• Harbour Act
Railway Station	• Fulfilment of simple transportation and distribution functions • Abolition of freight yards within an inner urban area	• Acceleration of land use • Transportation hub through transfer centre establishment • Provision of rental housing in an inner urban	• Urban Development Act Railroad • Construction Act • Railroad Safety Act
Relocated Site	• Formerly public organisations, military facilities and abandoned factories	• Maximise the value through integrated development • Reuse the areas for culture, education and parks	
Use of Local Assets	• Underutilised heritage and cultural assets of community	• Attract tourists and floating population by encouraging culture and tourism businesses	• Special Act for promoting a traditional market and shopping district

Source: MOLIT website (n.d.), and SAUR in Article 2 (2013) [re-organised and translated by author]

As an example of how the above operated in practice and how the initiatives called for partnership working, in Busan, seven Ministries participated in the various projects, each had different approaches and purposes. In addition, each Ministry had different responsibilities covering their own specialities and expertise, for example, [Ministry of Environment] creates ecology playground and restores project of a river in the urban area, [Ministry of Culture, Sports and Tourism] supports for local artists, and long-term activation of resident participation through cultural activities, [Cultural Heritage Administration] discovers and creates the cultural heritage and tourism assets, [Ministry of Government Administration and Home Affairs] encourages a community enterprise and improves the walking environment, [Ministry of Science, ICT and Future Planning] manages the creative economy innovation centre, [Ministry of Employment and Labour] creates local employment such as start-up incubator business, finds and encourages local artists, and [Ministry of Oceans and Fisheries, and Busan Port Authority] renews project of the Busan North harbour and promotes pedestrian-tech businesses. With regards to financial support, $25bn was injected by central and local government to create a public park, a car park, an extended road, proper public facilities and essential infrastructure in 2014. In addition, designated areas can receive benefits from deregulation by, for instance, lessening restrictions pertaining to floor area ratios, building to land ratios, height limits, and tax reduction or exemptions.

II. Social-led Regeneration Approach at Central and Community Levels

The social-led regeneration approach includes a rich variety of local experiences and perceptions. It is also notable that they tend to place greater emphasis on the improvement of localities and encouraging community contribution than economic-led regeneration schemes. These initiatives aim to create wider neighbourhood improvements and work with local people to articulate community needs. The schemes began in 2014 and can be split into the central and community levels by choosing 11 areas as pioneering projects. In terms of the central area, it targets the area of the central shopping district in decline and the relocated sites of public organisations using $20 billion. And the residential district and local market areas are designated as a community level with funding of $10 billion.

The advent of social-led regeneration aims to create property and socio-economic improvements (MOLIT website, n.d.) and is more focused on improving the social conditions within deprived communities and encouraging social cohesion, boosting social capital, and promoting community involvement. There are key programmes involved within social-led regeneration, depending on the scale that is targeted:

Central areas

- Create an artist or creative place with public parking space through investment in empty or unused shops
- Expand or remodel fundamental infrastructure
- Launch local festivals
- Revitalise traditional markets

Community units

- Develop the essential infrastructure for daily life such as designated fire vehicle access route, parking, health care centres, libraries and parks
- Promote small-sized home improvement businesses.
- Produce the opportunity to create income through local enterprises such as cooperative associations or local markets.
- Repair deteriorating buildings (e.g. roof and wall repairs, building structural reinforcements)

Social-led regeneration at the central level usually requires a higher level of private investment and more economic revitalisation than projects at a community level. These initiatives seek to develop a community's ability to engage in the local economy. As part of the schemes, urban regeneration co-ordinators are trained and dispatched to the targeted communities to connect the public sector, private organisations and local residents. Urban regeneration-related education programmes (e.g. urban regeneration university[2], refer to reference) can also be created for residents and become a supportive way to reinforce awareness of urban regeneration schemes, and encourage the active participation of residents.

III. Neighbourhood-led Urban Regeneration (Saddlemauel Project)

The principal purpose of a neighbourhood-led regeneration approach is to deliver local employment opportunities, community training programmes, small-scale property development, and basic infrastructure improvement. There is a wide range of small projects that are covered under this classification, including fence repairs, the building of shared homes, community business promotions, converting vacant homes into rental properties, and providing community

---

[2] Urban Regeneration University: The program actually focuses on attracting local resident participation and educational program for recognition of urban regeneration project. All of participants could plan the regeneration initiative by receiving professional help from experts.

infrastructure (such as common toilets, laundries and workplaces). Target areas should meet three criteria: i) be a poor neighbourhood without fundamental infrastructures, ii) contain households struggling with minimum f living standards, and iii) be a congested area with second-class citizens (See Table 3-6).

The Saddlemauel project, launched in 2015 and was given a four-year fund of $2 billion to $5 billion, is one example of how this approach can work. The project proceeded alongside economic and social-led regeneration schemes, with a particular focus on isolated areas (e.g. the shanty towns and the hinterlands of industrial complexes).

Table 3-6. Types and features of Saddlemaeul Project

Types	Features
Poor Hillside Village	• Congested area by refugee settlement • Vulnerable safety (e.g. hilly land and landslide) • Insufficient supply about sewerage, electricity and gas
Doss house in city	• Immigrant settlement by demolition • Low-income groups at the Japanesque building
Hinterland of industrial complex	• Settlement of low-income industrial workers • Vulnerable to noise, rubbish, and disturbance • Mix of immigrant worker and low-income groups
Run-down residential area	• Limited development district • Declined residential area by renewal project cancellation • Vulnerable residential area by hollowing out the urban area

Source: MOLIT (2015). [Re-organised and translated by author]

Thus, the SAUR provides direct guidance and strategic planning at local and community levels than before. It also has three overarching key themes to stabilise the urban regeneration system, including economic-led, social-led (central and community areas), and neighbourhood-led regenerations. However, the current regeneration initiative has faced challenges, for instance, solving the pre-investing expense of previous urban redevelopment projects, treating the revocation areas by the failure of the urban redevelopment project, and recognising the social needs of communities. Furthermore, providing empowerment to local residents in the decision-making process remains a critical point that has not been adequately addressed. Biased decision-making by civil servants, stakeholders, politicians, elite groups and experts can marginalise local community voices.

3.4. Summary

This chapter has traced policy shifts from urban redevelopment and new town projects to a more people-based regeneration approach. Forcible demolitions brought irreversible damage to areas which then suffered from cancelled projects. The shift to various forms of urban regeneration has tackled a range of problems related to these thoughtless demolitions, loss of urban amenity, the displacement of communities, and social exclusion. However, there are still questions that remain unanswered with regards to engagement with marginalised communities and whether the social aspects of urban regeneration receive adequate recognition. By examining urban redevelopment processes, it is apparent that social issues (e.g. quality of life, human rights, local empowerment, and community inclusion) are frequently neglected. If the top-down decision-making processes imposed by civil servants, politicians, elite groups and large-scale firms are continuously utilised in processes of urban regeneration, new regenerative projects may replicate past mistakes.

Chapter 4

Arts and Culture and Urban Regeneration

in South Korea

The previous chapter explored the development of urban redevelopment initiatives and urban regeneration strategy in general. In this chapter, I seek to situate those debates and examine the context for culturally informed regeneration in South Korea. It is important to consider how cultural elements (e.g. festivals, programmes and mega-events) have been adopted to develop communities and the city, alongside examining the attempts and challenges of current culture-led regeneration strategies. This chapter starts with a discussion of the history of cultural policy within the context of urban planning, and how cultural policies and initiatives have been integrated into the urban regeneration process. Thereafter the chapter examines individual cultural examples which have been adopted after the legislation of the SAUR in 2013. As noted, given the short history of culture-led urban regeneration in South Korea, there is little empirical evidence to underpin existent academic literature. Therefore, the chapter includes views from urban experts who were interviewed during the field-research in 2015 and 2016, as well as articles from newspapers and other secondary sources.

4.1. The History of Cultural Policies within the Context of Urban Planning

There have been a number of changes within the cultural policies of South Korea. Indeed, there have been 112 different laws relating to culture and the arts within the country, covering cultural heritage and history, cultural industry, broadcasting, and the media. In order to briefly understand these laws, this section examines the development of government policies surrounding these issues.

An important starting point for thinking about the integration of culture and urban policy in South Korea is the 'Culture and Arts Promotion Act' which was passed in 1972 under the government of Park Chung-hee. The intention of the Act was to formulate and manage a long-term cultural development plan, and it can be considered as the essential structuring starting point for the culture and arts of South Korea (Kim, 1976). As the fundamental law for arts and culture, it followed model German-Austrian law in stressing the state's role in encouraging arts and culture (Kulturfoederungesetz) (Hong, 2013). The government of Park

Chung-hee centred priorities on economic growth and provided proactive cultural policies by establishing laws, institutions, organisations and public funds. In particular, on 19 October 1973, the government of Park announced the first 'Five-Year Plan for Promotion of Culture' to bring a cultural renaissance by forming a new national culture based on traditional culture between 1974 and 1978. This plan focused on three broad areas: traditional culture (history, conventional arts, and cultural properties), contemporary arts (literature, fine arts, music, drama, and dance), and popular culture (cinema and publishing) which were the prerequisite for the creation of a new South Korean culture. The Act was the inaugural comprehensive long-term plan for cultural policy, and 70% of the total public expenditure spent on the plan was distributed to the o arts and traditional culture during the period between 1974 and 1978 d (Ministry of Culture and Information, 1979).

During the 1970s, the key objectives of cultural policy were the promotion of people's active participation in the field of culture and the arts. Cultural policies have been increasingly developed since the 1980s. In particular, the central government started to invest large sums into establishing cultural infrastructures (such as the Seoul Arts Centre), and on expanding tangible infrastructure. Local governments were financially backed by the central government to establish new cultural facilities including theatres, public libraries, galleries and museums. However, the 1980's cultural policy system was a "Grands Travaux type of policy resulting in art centres that were monotonous in design and function, and which did not reflect local cultural identity. Unbalanced growth between hardware and software, the results were also disappointing. Local governments were ill-equipped to run programmes in those facilities" (Hong, 2013a). The policy was more concerned with creating economic benefits than preserving cultural heritage and the traditional arts of the country.

The economic importance of cultural policies was intensified in the early 1990s through a period of interurban competition for economic development promoted by the central government. In line with the growing competition between local governments, arts and culture played a catalysing role for city marketing through the hosting of local festivals and cultural activities, alongside the building of grade-scale cultural facilities. After the 1990s, the use of cultural policies and planning policies as tools for urban development in the metropolitan cities of South Korea was highlighted through the Liberal Roh Moo Hyun government (2002-2008). The cultural city project, which aimed to balance national land development and encourage decentralisation, was introduced to boost urban cultural policies. Specifically, Gwangju (the sixth-largest city in South Korea and the Capital of South Jeolla Province) was chosen to become a 'Hub City of Asian Culture', and the project was planned to last from 2004 to 2023 as the first long-term national project in the culture and arts field (Park, 2005). It was South Korea's most ambitious cultural facility development to date and included a mega-size cultural venue, the Asian Cultural Complex, a Cultural Exchange, and an Asian Culture Information unit (Fisher, 2014). The cultural city project gradually expanded and the Ministry of Culture and Tourism aimed to "have implemented a cultural policy of renovating several mid-sized cities such as Gwangju, Kyongju and Jeonju as international cultural cities" in response to global market demands (Lee, 2007, p.1). 'Historical-Cultural City in Kyongju', 'Visual Entertainment City in Busan', 'Traditional Cultural City in Jeonju', and 'Entertainment City in Incheon emerged in the early 2000s. As long-term national projects, they are still in progress, but there have been considerable conflicts as government priorities have frequently changed. There have been criticisms pertaining to the disappearance of the initial purposes of the scheme, the improper appointment of directors, the existence of result-oriented bureaucracy management, and the interruption of building construction. For example, one planned building (called the Democracy Peace Exchange Centre) was neglected as civic groups claimed it would destroy historical resources during construction, and it remained an eyesore until 2016. Another criticism revolves around claims that the cultural city project was a political project which failed to consider other cultural industries or participants.

4.2. Cultural Elements in Local Development Strategies and their social impacts

Despite the problems associated with the cultural city project, many cities sought to launch their own cultural policies and strategies in the early 2000s. Beyond the application of culture in large-scale projects, there have been various small and medium-sized cultural attempts at the local or community level. In this regard, 'Liveable Community Projects' (hereafter, LCP) were officially institutionalised by the central government in 2005 and incorporated numerous cultural programmes (such as festivals, education programmes, and culture and arts projects) into a single policy stream. The LCPs began to intervene and tackle the social problems of declining areas (such as poor dwellings, welfare, lack of work, and low-quality environments, as well as issues pertaining to poor health and safety issues) through cultural interventions. The use of culture within the LCPs became an essential prerequisite for developing a declining city or community, and the LCPs became the cornerstone of current culture-led urban regeneration initiatives. A total of 57 pioneer areas were accepted for the LCP programmes between 2007 and 2009. Three, in particular, are useful to examine in detail to explore and establish how cultural policies have become integrated with urban policies. These three areas sought to preserve local culture through bottom-up strategies that encouraged citizen participation. They are the projects that were cited in the villages of Hanok in Jeonju, Seongmisan in Seoul and Samdeok in Daegu.

Table 4-1. Representative cultural projects in three villages

I) Hanok Village in Jeonju

Hanok (traditional Korean house) is a village in Jeonju. The project has integrated old and modern cultures to allow for the preservation of tradition while simultaneously attempting to invigorate the area (Yu, 2012). Hanok village was selected as a pioneer area for the LCPs between 2007 and 2009, as the area has more than 800 Korean traditional houses with the potential for cultural preservation and development. During the 1970s, the village faced decline as the intensified growth of the urban area forced manufacturing industries to move to the suburbs (Korea Research Institute for Human Settlements, 2012, hereafter KRIHS). To alleviate the village's problems, the LCP implemented several initiatives, such as the preservation of Hanok structure and traditional sports (e.g. Korean wrestling, Pitch-pot, driving a hoop, and so on.), employing traditional and local cultural guides, food festivals, music festivals and creating local products and foods. The consistent cultural efforts and the creation of a variety of creative ideas allowed the village to become the most famous tourist attraction in South Korea. Hanok village attracted a record number of tourists in 2017; over 10 million people, a 10% increase on 2015 (9 million) (Kim, 2017). It was identified that preserving and developing local traditional cultural resources could be the most efficacious means of making a successful competitive city.

II) Seongmisan Village in Seoul

Seongmisan village is located within the city of Seoul. The area is well-known as a cooperative village that operates well within its urban surroundings (Yu, 2012). Residents created location-based solidarity through encouraging participation and collaboration with community projects. This initially began in 1994 with 20 couples who, unable to access suitable childcare, banded together to raise their own. They invested in a childcare centre (which was the first cooperative childcare facility in South Korea), and opened a cooperative after-school centre in 1999. The cooperative philosophy has been boosted and advanced by hosting an annual festival since May 2001, and the opening of the Sungmisan Village Theatre in 2009. The village expanded its cultural offerings through the LCP program in 2007 with a focus on cultural education, workshops, car-sharing, and creating affiliations between support organisation and vulnerable social groups for enhancing the local environment and improving residents' life. The cultural program under the LCPs added to the area's cultural prosperity (Korea Research Institute for Human Settlements (hereafter, KRIHS), 2012) and all culture-related programs are ongoing. One unique feature of this village is that there are no franchised restaurants and cafes which can sometimes be a criterion in the evaluation success or failure of culture and arts strategies. The case of Seongmisan shows that the co-operation of residents and consistent investment in culture can have a considerable impact in attracting people, investment and creating sustainability.

III) Samdeok Village in Daegu

Samdeok village in Daegu is a representative case of the bottom-up approach in South Korea. In 1997, the support centre for runaway teenagers was established (now used as a craft shop) in Samdeok village, despite furious resident resistance because of potential safety and crime issues (Lee and Kim, 2016). At the time, one resident in support of the centre destroyed the wall of his house to create a shared communication space between teenagers and local residents in 1998. The shared space positively triggered the creation of small-gardens, arts exhibition spaces and cultural performance areas, operating within the newly created open spaces. Since then there a mobile library, community mural painting and other cultural events within the village have been created and held. The efforts of Samdeok villagers received further momentum after the area was designated as an LCP; funds went towards space design projects, street artworks (e.g. repairs of mural painting, artistic work installation, the establishment of a community theatre, hosting a puppet pantomime festival and rearrangement of a community gallery), and cultural education programs for residents (e.g. opening the football club, an adult arts school, a library club, and traditional instrument classes for young people). Such a bottom-up approach (led by residents) attracted government support and blocked the invasion of urban redevelopment initiatives – Samdeok village was designated as an urban redevelopment area in 2016, but the village was not demolished by the redevelopment initiative.

As this book focuses on the social regeneration factors that arise from the cultural approach, it is important to reflect on the social impacts of these three case studies. In the case of Hanok village in Jeonju, the cultural effects were evident through the preservation and development of local traditions which fostered local cultural capability (KRIHS, 2012) and created a voluntary willingness amongst residents to further enhance their material surroundings. This created a form of attachment from residents to their local community, creating a snowball effect in which they tied themselves to the conservation of local traditions and culture. As the degree of satisfaction about the cultural program in the village grew, creative ideas were constantly produced amongst the residents as well as merchants of Hanok village. Although some people criticised the radical commercialisation of traditional cultural resources, residents' perceptions about culture and art investments to the village are fairly high and positive.

In Seongmisan village (known as a co-operative village), the resident protest against the urban redevelopment initiative led to a community-based cultural event which worked to strengthen relationships and co-operation between residents (Human and Community, 2012). The Seongmisan community theatre, opened and funded by the LCPs, still provides a plentiful program (e.g. youth theatre, community theatre, traditional arts, play, cinema, workshop, elderly cultural program), and has been mainly managed and operated by residents). One of the theatre's leading residents said:

> "Community is the world. Seongmisan residents enjoy talking each other, share the common interest and creative ideas, play together, sing their dream and bring up child together. Also, the Seongmisan theatre is the place to celebrate and share all the community issues in different ways such as theatre, bazaar, playing musicals, exhibition, etc.".

To the residents of Seongmisan village, the cultural and arts resources created through constant co-operative efforts to develop the community are prized assets. Community employment added to social and community value: for example, there are more than 150 people working at the Childcare Centre, Seongmisan School, the Consumer Cooperative and the Theatre to protect and preserve the village (Yu, 2012). As the number of clubs for cultural and arts activities (e.g. Seongmisan Pungmul Band (Korean traditional percussion band), a photography club, a video club, a middle-aged rock band and a village choral group) has grown, residents feel more satisfied than before, and the quality of cultural education for young people is growing.

Finally, in Samdeok village in Daegu, as many neighbours and public buildings participated destroyed their walls and unlocked space for public use, the places became filled with rich cultural resources (Lim, 2015). The bottom-up approach and co-operative nature of residents enhanced self-esteem and created a joint responsibility amongst the same for preserving the community. Moreover, the participation of residents in community design and street artworks, the opening of a community gallery and the management of puppet shows have created a positive change in perceptions towards culture and the area, increasing volunteering awareness, and improving community cohesion (Kim, 2015).

4.3. The Cultural Implications of Mega-events:
The Gwangju Biennale and the 2012 Yeosu Expo

As this book uses large-scale events to develop an understanding of the wider context of culture-led urban regeneration aspects, it is useful to examine the impacts of mega-events on city development (e.g. economy and tourist growth) and the potential improvement that such social factors (e.g. cultural perception, community enhancement and residents' living environment) bring. There is no doubt that many metropolitan cities in South Korea have sought to host mega-cultural events to revitalise and promote their cities within the competitive era. This type of event is, however, often only part of a broader cultural policy whereby a city seeks to enhance an image or reputation through a concentration of various and well-known cultural events during a certain period of time. Sometimes, such cultural strategies lead to the discovery of new driving forces within the local economy through the provision of cultural consumption, and new ways of rebranding a city as a cultural destination. To explain these issues, two examples – The Gwangju Biennale and the Yeosu Expo – are examined in this section.

I) The Gwangju Biennale

The city of Gwangju, lying to the southwest of South Korea, has been marketed as the representative birthplace of democracy since 1980. The democratic uprising in Gwangju is considered as a pivotal moment within the nation's history, and the protest retains an unsavoury image of the ' city of resistance', 'a city of democracy', and even 'a city of blood'. To change the image of the city, Gwangju was keen to transform the city through top-down approaches, so that it could move beyond political images to one of being a vibrant cultural city. To achieve this, the local government created the cultural festival of 'Gwangju Biennale' in 1995 (Shin and Stevens, 2013). The Gwangju Biennale had the initial aim of reinvigorating the cultural and historical places within the city (e.g. the Gwangju theatre, traditional market, and 5/18 memorial park) through displaying well-known artworks and cultural programmes. The purpose was to create a vibrant and memorable cultural attraction to visitors, and its cultural efforts had gradually delivered widespread impacts. So, the city's revised reputation became the anchor by which it attracted the national cultural city project in 2004.

As a brief example, during the 2002 Biennale, an abandoned railway was transformed and filled with artistic works – such as recycled sculptures, drawing exhibitions, an open-space museum, plantings to develop the urban economy. A total of 23 artists and a number of residents provided their ideas and time to transform the deserted railway converting the disused tracks into a successful new oasis for citizens and visitors. Another example occurred in 2008, when the deprived traditional market was revitalised by offering space to local or external artists. As the Biennale attracted creative and talented artists, their works drew visitors to the declining traditional market area. The endeavours were not just confined to showing off artists' works but also included facilitating interactions between cultural production and the enjoyment of ordinary people, as well as increasing the number of cultural tourists alongside traditional market visitors. Since 2016, the Biennale has heavily emphasised two key words – local embeddedness and social participation. To achieve this art's relevancy in the local community of Gwangju was added as the top priority. The biennale has attempted to involve Gwangju residents by hosting monthly gatherings, schooling projects, artistic screenings and curated walk around the city.

A criticism of the project revolves around the state-sponsored market cultural scheme becoming too commercially focused with too much of an emphasis on economic growth, rather than cultural value and social cohesion (Joo, Bae, and Kassens-Noor, 2017). Many art critics also point out that the Biennale lost its primacy in preserving the locality with the internationalisation of events following the trends of globalisation. Furthermore, as the elites and civil servants have been actively involved in various Biennale programmes, the Biennale producers tend to regard the general audience and residents as merely passive consumers. Such actions have generated widespread apathy for the Biennale amongst. Residents. In terms of public involvement, the bureaucratic characteristic of the mega-event has obstructed and restricted residents' voice and participation in the decision-making process, although the Biennale still emphasises its active social participation processes. One argument is that the Biennale should more fully take into account the needs of residents and the local community rather than predominantly focusing on attracting visitors and investment.

II) The Yeosu Expo in 2012

The second example of a cultural mega-event is the Yeosu Expo which was hosted in 2012 under the theme of 'The Living Ocean and Coast' and attracted 104 participating countries. Yeosu is located on the southern coast of South Korea in the South Jeolla Province and is well-known as the most picturesque port city in the country. As the city boasts an international ocean resort, it has become a principle tourist destination for overseas visitors. As part of the wider gradual process of urban development, the Yeosu Expo was the catalyst to promote Yeosu as a cultural city. The initial intention of the Yeosu Expo was the development of the provincial city through cultural activities. The preparation period took four years, and £6.2bn was invested to start the event. A total of 104 nations and 10 international organisations participated in stage exhibitions which consisted of 80 pavilions and a large aquarium on a 25-ha area for three months. As a result, the Expo attracted nearly 8 million visitors with 400 programmes and presented more than 8,000 performances (Guideline for EXPO 2012 Yeosu Korea, n.d.). In terms of cultural tourism, the expo was a powerful instrument for tourism development: for example, more than 100 hotel rooms, 5 resorts and luxurious accommodations were newly established or renovated to accommodate visitors. Furthermore, this mega-event was beneficial in promoting the city as a cultural city.

However, Yeosu Expo has received more criticism than positive feedback with regards to issues of management, the prediction of audience numbers, and promotion methods used (Hankyoreh, 2012). The Yeosu Expo report officially published the number of attendants as being over 8 million people during the Expo, but during Expo's final four days tickets were given away for free to attract 270,000 visitors to meet the final target. Secondly, the Yeosu Expo provoked an increase in living costs, taxes and property values that generated economic difficulties for local residents. The cost of living index, for example, became the highest in the country during the Expo. In this situation, local businesses struggled with the economic recession, and the population suffered from enhanced urban sprawl.

The third problem was that the Yeosu Expo lost its purpose and meaning after suffering a lower rate of revenue than that which had been expected, low attendance numbers, and a lack of programme arrangements (Kim, 2012). To achieve its tangible purpose, the Expo organisation hosted famous singers as a key driver to attract more audience – an activity not included as an original aim. This led, to criticism that the organisation had lost its key focus. There was an escalation in the self-confidence of citizens and an elevation of local status; however, a confusion of policy, the wrong estimates of audience numbers, the lack of an adequate transportation structure, and the failure of a local business strategy all became key criticisms. Finally, the most important challenge of the Expo to date is that it has failed to offer a sustainable ex post facto management for the newly built infrastructure. As Jones and Evans (2008, p.138) emphasise, "the buildings are only as successful as the uses to which they are put, and high-profile flops have left some areas with embarrassing and very expensive white elephants", for which sustainable uses have yet to be discovered.

4.4. Interactions between Cultural Strategy and Urban Policy in Urban Regeneration Initiatives Since 2013

As the SAUR began its interventions in earnest, culture and the arts have undoubtedly been key drivers for local development. This section details and reviews the value of promoting culture to enhance regeneration, and the involvement of practical, cultural works since the SAUR became a fundamental policy in South Korea. In 2014, 86 local areas applied to the bid of urban regeneration projects, and 13 areas were chosen amongst them. The selected cities emphasised embracing an intermediary, distributive and innovative project to generate vitality in economic and social aspects of an area. In order to implement, culture related strategies (from architecture to artistic works and cultural events) were mainly considered as an effective instrument. As shown in Table 4-2, 13 areas were designated as regeneration pioneering areas over four-years from 2014, and of those, 9 areas incubated strategies of fostering cultural resources and creating cultural quarters.

Table 4-2. The specific regeneration strategies in 2014, South Korea

Types	Local governments		Target neighborhoods	Businesses strategies
Economic-led	Busan	Dong-gu*	- Choryang-dong	Creative economy cluster around the Busan harbour and train station
	Chung-buk*	Cheongju	- Naedeok-dong - Uam-dong - Jungang-dong	Craft and cultural quarters at the former tobacco factory
Social-led	Seoul	Jongro-gu	- Sungin-dong - Changsin-dong	Regeneration within residential areas where were designated as a revocation area of the New Town
	Gwangju	Dong-gu	- Chungjang-dong - Dongmyeong-dong - Sansu-dong - Jisan-dong	Revitalisation of local businesses around the Asia cultural centre
	Jeon-buk	Gunsan	- Wolmyeong-dong - Haesin-dong - Jungang-dong	Creating a historical district within the harbour area
	Jeon-nam*	Mokpo	- Mokwon-dong	Making artist village using a deserted or un-used buildings and houses
	Kyeong-buk	Yeongju	- Yeongju-dong	Boosting the ability of traditional market in vicinity and station
	Kyeong-nam	Changwon	- Dongseo-dong - Seongho-dong - Odong-dong	Harbour renaissance project and enhancing culture-led urban regeneration strategy around Changdong arts town
	Daegu	Nam-gu	- Daemyeong-dong	Creation of cultural theatre street with 100 small theatres
	Kwang-won	Taebaek	- Tongdong	Regeneration of cultural and historical sites (e.g. coal mine area and abandoned railways)
	Chung-nam	Cheonan	- Jungang-dong - Munseon-dong	Creation of basic infrastructure for youngsters at un-used buildings (e.g. accommodation, art studios, etc.)
	Chung-nam	Gongju	- Ungjin-dong - Junghak-dong - Okryong-dong	Creating the historical quarter about Baekje era, and development of the traditional market
	Jeon-nam	Suncheon	- Hyang-dong - Jungang-dong	Making of environment-friendly village in a run-down area

Source: http://www.molit.go.kr/USR/WPGE0201/m_35396/DTL.jsp
* **Buk** means north of the province, and **Nam** is south of the province
* **Gu** represents districts

Within the culture-led urban regeneration process, several specified cultural resources were delivered at a variety of different scales; from large-scale projects (such as the creation of cultural cluster at a harbour or train station,) to small local-based projects (such as the revitalisation of a historical site). In terms of budgetary planning, the costs varied depending on the type of economic-led or social-led regeneration utilised. Generally, central government supported 50% of national expenses, for example, an area chosen as an economic-led regeneration initiative could receive $25 billion from the central government, while a social-regeneration designated area could receive $10 billion (MOLIT website, n.d.). In terms of practical implementation, many projects have been carried out in the designated pioneering cities since 2014. Representative examples are explained IN Table NUMBER - SPECIFIC

Table 4-3. Examples of practical implementation based on culture and arts

---

I) Mokpo in Jeonam

In Mokpo in Jeonnam, 17 cultural interpreters were employed to introduce and explain the local culture, as well as the area's historic sites and artistic works to visitors. To support this strategy, the Jeonnam government enthusiastically encouraged street tours to attract more cultural tourists and offered various cultural opportunities. In June 2017, the culture and arts enterprise project launched by the local offered 50 places to cultural projects, including office spaces, unused houses and part of a building to enhance a street's vitality. And it had various projects from craft, exhibition, photography, performance, design and drawing to food, service and IT. Several benefits were also offered, such as subsidies for business management to aid the remodelling of office space and 50% rental fee support for two years.

II) Changsin-dong in Seoul

The case of Changsin-dong, Seoul, (Known as the birthplace of the sewing industry), has been culturally eligible for preservation. In the context of culture-led urban regeneration, the overriding aim was to protect the local historical asset without brutal demolition. The local area aimed to foster a local cultural legacy. For example, the representative local artists 'Nam-jun Baek (Korean American artist, and founder of video art)', and Su-gen Park (Korean painter)' have been culturally symbolised through the public artworks in this area. $2.7 billion was also invested to support historic culture through establishing a memorial space for Nam-jun Baek, the development of story-telling to explain local cultural resources, and support for local artists.

III) Wolmyeong-dong in Gunsan

The initial aims were to preserve the area's modern architecture and revitalise local businesses through cultural intervention. In order to realise these aims, the area was designated as a thematic street which incorporated the cultural assets of the opening port era. The regeneration strategy promoted the creation of design-specialised buildings and maritime parks. Specifically, for the creation of design buildings, a maximum rental limit was coordinated by the land-owner, the cultural organisation and the urban regeneration centre. This means that if a land-owner offers a space or an office for around a £1,300 deposit and less than a £130 monthly rental fee, culture-related businesses (such as local museums, galleries,) can use the space to host various cultural programmes. As a result of this cultural strategy, the number of tourists visiting local museums has substantially escalated from 820,000 in 2015 to 1,020,000 in 2016, with the numbers of shops increasing from 437 to 456 (Jung, 2017).

4.5. The Challenges of Culture-led Urban Regeneration in South Korea

Although there are a number of positive effects from culture-led urban regeneration schemes, criticisms are inevitable. In general, many culture-led regeneration projects are weighted towards the development of flagship buildings and through the infusion of unsystematic cultural programmes for achieving stakeholders' goals in the short-term. In addition, the regeneration schemes of South Korea tend to benchmark and follow successful examples from other countries. However, they are not always suitably adopted to fit within local contexts. Firstly, the loss of locality is a considerable concern. In the case of Gwangju (see section 4.2.), a significant cultural transformation has been ongoing for operating the cultural city project, a lot of the focus has been heavily centred on constructing the symbolic cultural building. However, the adjacent areas and needed improvements to the wider urban environment are often neglected. The project had the initial idea to regenerate the surrounding urban areas, but the focusing on a single symbolic building led to arguments that the project had lost its local characteristics, and promoted external franchises and high street luxury brands within shopping areas at the expense of local businesses. Therefore, it has been criticised as neglecting Gwangju's own history and philosophy, with the culture-led regeneration projects seeking to produce a result within a short time.

Secondly, the lack of effective partnerships which occurred in Cheongju where has resulted in unexpected outcomes with regards to attracting private partnerships. Cheongju was chosen as the economic-led regeneration target area in 2014. The former Tobacco Factory was designated for revival as a cultural complex within the regeneration strategy. After the factory was closed in 2004, urban decline gradually fed into the surrounding residential areas, and several neighbourhoods raised concerns as to the derelict factory leading to crime, and juvenile delinquency. To tackle the problems and drive regeneration, cultural strategies (such as the establishment of National Museum Contemporary Art,), and attracting knowledge industries such as R&D and electronic commerce were planned for the Tobacco Factory. In the process of attracting private investment, Cheongju attempted to encourage private involvement; however, there was no one in charge of investment and scheme was considered to be a poor business possibility (Yeonhapnews, 2016). Due to this, the city made an effort to consult again with the Ministry of Land, Infrastructure and Transport regarding the approach that should be taken with regard to the Tobacco Factory's regeneration. As a result, Cheongju decided to provide authority to a private company to determine future strategies. Moreover, Cheongju suggested removing restrictions on the types of regeneration that could be allowed on the site. This led to criticisms that accepting and entrusting a private company's preferences might provoke ambiguous results and large capital circulation.

Thirdly, culture-led urban regeneration caused difficulties for entrepreneurs and local business. In Cheonan, as the regeneration project was heavily centred on stakeholders' purposes, a number of entrepreneurs and local businesses struggled. Under the terms of the culture-led regeneration project, local cultural organisations (such as independent galleries) may be threatened by the building of new galleries or the signature cultural centre. In addition, the head of the Cheonan youth centre argued that large companies and the government sometimes use the initial items and ideas created by young entrepreneurs by investing a large sum of money in the process of culture-led regeneration. This leads to creative young people working elsewhere and away from cultural areas. In this sense, many artistic opportunities for young people have been divested under the terms of culture-led regeneration.

Finally, as culture and arts can attract many visitors, a sudden influx of people causes a certain loss of residential privacy and excessive noise and rubbish around such areas. For instance, before the SAUR was legislated, colourful murals and art installations were spread out and helped to beautify slum areas. Since 2006, the adoption of mural painting became a cultural strategy in the small village of Dongpirang in the Sothern coastal city of Tongyeong. The murals significantly impacted the area's internal economic growth and resulted in a re-imagination of village life. As the village has seen the rising popularity of the mural paintings as a tourist attraction, many local governments have adopted the concept of mural painting or public art installation scheme to revitalise areas in need of development (e.g. Ihwa-dong in Seoul / Yeomri-dong in Seoul / Haenggung-dong in Suwon / Songwol-dong, Incheon, and so on).

At first, artworks can be seen as charming and contribute to the creation of a vibrant environment in a depressed area. However, many of the artworks have been spoiled by visitors, and broken works are often neglected by the artists and local government. Such spoiled artworks have become an eyesore in many communities and particularly led to the community's segmentation by immoderate mural painting acceptance. It has meant that a number of residents have complained about the artworks. Indeed, someone covered the mural with grey paint and wrote 'we want to live like a human', 'desperately oppose of culture-led regeneration project', 'please be quiet', 'the invasion of tourist in a village'. This created tensions between communities. The abandoned artistic works and people's aggressive complaints generated a more violent atmosphere and an image of an area which was hostile to outsiders.

Despite various problems with mural painting such as residential privacy, a lack of sustainability, and the creation of improper artworks that ignore local characteristics, many culture-led regeneration initiatives have adopted mural painting works as an essential cultural strategy. It is argued that planners and organisers should reflect upon these works carefully when attempting to adopt similar schemes. Shaw (2016, p.272) suggests that "mural art is used to speak in the name of and depict communities, nations and cultures, as well as to represent an aesthetic element which helps them integrate into their environments". The longevity, legacy, and the creativity of local people as well as issues pertaining to the local environment must also be reflected when adopting mural painting scheme as a culture-led urban regeneration strategy. The plethora of artworks is hardly a solution to revitalise a slum or deprived area: the area's cultural value as well as creating opportunities for collaborations between local government, artists and residents should be the priorities culture-led regeneration processes.

4.6. Experts' Perspectives of Culture-led Urban Regeneration Challenges

This section explains how South Korean urban planning experts consider and manage culture-led regeneration. This section aids an understanding of the current circumstances of culture-led regeneration in South Korea and also assists one to identify what the problematic contemporary issues are.

As shown in Figure 4-1, the current concerns which experts have about culture-led regeneration in South Korea are: the bureaucratic top-down approach, the loss of locality, the fact that it is an outcome-oriented system, the inappropriate arrangement of cultural programmes, the impact and furtherance of gentrification, and the existence of an unstable public administration system.

Figure 4-1: The problems of the urban regeneration process in South Korea according to experts

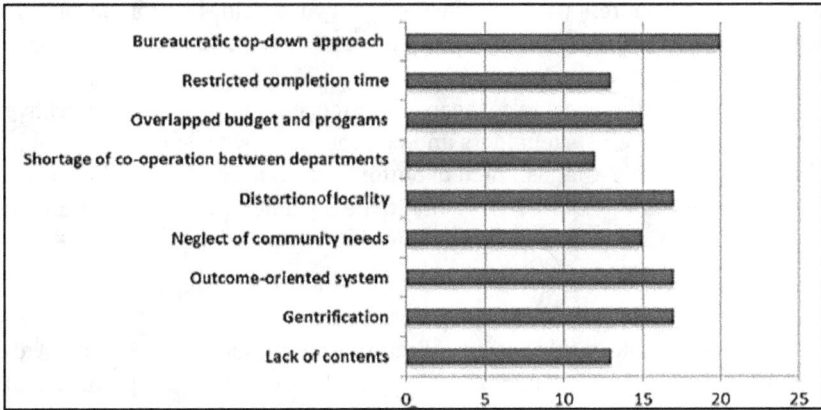

Source: author

Firstly, the intimate link between locals and their culture has been considered to be one of the most important factors in post-2000 urban regeneration (Hwang, 2015). If local characteristics are disrupted or destroyed, then the value of any urban area is meaningless. However, within the projects discussed in previous sections, the unique nature of each area has often been distorted by the bureaucratic and top-down policies established by the central government with its preferences to fund larger cultural projects. In the typical system of top-down urban planning in South Korea, the government normally outsources a number of planning works to maximise the use of external resources and streamline the efficiency of time-consuming functions. However, a city's unique geographical and local characteristics can be lost in this process. For example, a private companies' application of the same "model" of planning naturally omits the distinctive local features of an area. Current culture-led urban regeneration processes tend to generate a narrow perspective of 'franchising' of local characteristics within targeted areas.

Beyond the franchising of local characteristics, miscellaneous cultural imports and the simple replication of examples of around the world often means that local cultural features take a back seat. For instance, if the central government allocates $70 billion for improving a city's environment within a short time frame, local governments and outsourcing companies normally focus on building a single mega-sized and symbolic facility without any consideration as to the need to ensure that it harmonises with the surrounding local area and traditional characteristics (Hwang, 2015; Kwon, 2015). This is because the commercialisation and commodification of local culture are given an immediate high priority in the regenerative schemes of South Korea. Hwang

(2015) argues that it is still questionable as to "why South Korea's regeneration strategy does not focus on creating our own planning ecology". Kwon (2015) and Kim (2015a) stress that top-down s by city authorities may replicate the earlier mistakes of property-led redevelopment schemes. Moreover, there have not been appropriate opportunities for residents to engage in planning procedures and there has also been an absence of proper communicative approaches between stakeholders and communities by which to ensure that there is a systematic establishment of bottom-up strategies. It could be argued that the bottom-up approach is unattainable amongst the landscape of prevalent bureaucratic top-down systems.

The second concern is the outcome-oriented system. South Korea's public administration system normally requires projects to be hastened and hurried to create a tangible result within a limited time period (Kim, 2015b). With regard to culture-led regeneration, the prevalent outcome-oriented system means that local culture can be devalued. However, these circumstances have been considerably generalised within the processes of culture-led regeneration schemes in South Korea. An expert working at an architecture company commented that "outcome-oriented approach could not overcome the failure of urban redevelopment of new-town initiatives. 'Development-centred' and 'outcome-centred' theories in the urban planning of South Korea should be perished. If the stakeholders are constantly engrossed in achieving results, there are no long-term sustainable visions" (Hong, 2015).

Furthermore, a limited time period for quick completion could hamper attempts to provide adequate social provisions (such as support for living expenses, medical benefits, rental housing, and community development) according to Kim, (2015a). Hwang (2015) describes the typical outcome-oriented system in the process of culture-led regeneration as there are no people, but the business itself is solitarily left. Such circumstances have led to a polarisation of opinions between local interests with residents wanting to maintain the local economic structure, and the central government desiring to restrict the local economy through the creation of mega-sized cultural facilities within a restricted period. These conflicts are still controversial and contested issues in the process of culture-led regeneration (Hwang, 2015). Outcome-oriented systems and the time pressures created through state interventions have been increasingly created project 'stiffness'.

Third, the arrangement of various cultural programmes is a controversial problem in the process of culture-led regeneration. In general, a signature building is considered to be essential in implementing culture-led regeneration projects in many cities in South Korea (Kim, 2015b). Jones and Evans (2008, p. 126) emphasise that the "questions of whose culture is particularly important when considering schemes where a cultural facility is being used as an anchor for a larger regeneration programme". However, there are questions of what a landmark cultural iconic building actually says about a city, what impact it may have on existing local cultures, and the extent to which with the views and desires of local residents are hidden behind signature buildings. The inherent weaknesses of constructing a cultural anchor building in South Korea are a short-term fragmented, project-based, one-off and on ad hoc arrangement regardless to any inclusive strategic structure for community development (Jones and Evans, 2008; Hwang, 2015; Ahn, 2015). The proliferation of mural-painting within villages can be used as an example to demonstrate the shortage of appropriate cultural contents. One particular case of a mural painting-theme village must not become the prototype for all other cases. Not only it is extremely short-sighted, but this type of 'trendy' planning does very little to improve a community or preserve local identity and uniqueness (Jung, 2015). In this regard, mural painting contents are sometimes considered effortless work.

The causes of gentrification in culture-led regeneration in South Korea has been a long-running debate. To alleviate deprivation in declining areas, many local governments have eagerly attracted young and unique artists to assist in regeneration (Kwon, 2015). In Hongdae, Samcheong-dong, Seongsu-dong, and Moonrae-dong in Seoul, several artists created cultural spaces within unused building or warehouses located in a relatively cheap to buy deprived area. This phenomenon brought a large number of cultural consumers and investment to the area (Kim, 2015b). As the cultural quarter was popularly created, various private investments such as cafés, franchise restaurants and shopping complexes turned their attention to an area which had previously been overlooked. However, such a cultural influx can generate victims who live in culturally gentrifying areas and experience radical growth in rent, grocery prices and local services. It is also possible for the initial artists to be displaced and evicted by commercialisation because they are unable to afford the skyrocketing rental prices. Although gentrification can consider a phenomenon that occurs in the development process of cities, the 'culture departmentalisation phenomenon' is criticised as a social issue that harms local cultures in South Korea. According to this situation, just 'who the beneficiaries of culture-led regeneration' are, remains unanswered.

The final challenge of culture-led regeneration is the unstable public administration system of South Korea. The typical job rotation system of civil servants at central and local government levels has changed biennially. Practically, stable communication with private sectors, residents and voluntary organisations are pivotal to enabling regeneration initiatives to operate successfully. However, frequent rotation amongst staff within the public sector can cause a lack of coordination, as there is a need to constantly built new professional relationships relationship with different people and organisations. Such a public administration system results in uneven urban planning and unpredictable delays to projects (Hwang, 2015a; Koo, 2015). Another unreliable system is that current culture-led urban regeneration schemes have similar trends and policies that are operated by several different departments. For example, the Ministry of Land, Infrastructure and Transport has 17 regeneration strategies and Acts; the Ministry of Trade, Industry and Energy has 12 strategies; the Ministry of Public Administration and Security and the Ministry of Food, Agriculture, Forestry and Fisheries have 6 respectively; the Ministry of Culture, Sports and Tourism has 5; the Ministry of Environment has 4; the Ministry of Strategy and Finance and the Korea Forest Service have 2 respectively; the Regional Small and Medium Business Administration has 1; the Ministry of Education, Science and Technology and the Ministry of Defence, the Financial Services Commission and the Prime Minister's Office have 1 policy respectively. Such overlapping role and remit of public departments can also cause duplication of budgets, financial inefficiency, and inappropriate arrangements of cultural projects (Nam, 2012). Kim (2015a) suggested that urban regeneration projects are managed and planned by different Ministries, and even various departments at local government level also separately handle the regenerative projects. Therefore, grasping the current condition and which projects belong to which departments are significantly difficult. In addition, the dispersed nature of support offered by departments is constantly changing, and this makes it difficult to promote sustainable urban regeneration initiatives (Hong, 2015).

4.6. Summary

This chapter reviewed the changing relationship between the culture and arts and urban development in South Korea. It has shown how 'culture' has played an increasingly important role in regeneration activities linked to perceived economic benefits. However, the link to social aspects is more complicated. There has been social regeneration through the use of culture, but the extent to which culture has benefitted households facing multiple deprivations is still debatable. As can be seen from the view of academics, culture-led approaches in South Korea are often too top-down, with insufficient co-operation between departments. This results in a neglect of community needs, and criticism of inappropriate cultural activities being undertaken. Some cases (such as outcome-oriented system, top-down approach, outcome-oriented management) have led to significant gentrification and the displacement of residents as well as artists. In addition, the uncontrollable cultural influx has provoked residents' anger and complaints, and its reckless application has resulted in strong protests against cultural regeneration where the latter was felt to undermine the character and dynamics of villages.

Chapter 5

Understanding of Research Target Areas and Cultural Event (Cultural City of East Asia 2015)

To deeply explore the circumstance of culture-led urban regeneration in South Korea, this book focuses the culture-led regeneration initiatives and the CCEA – Cultural City of East Asia - which took place in 2015 in the city of Cheongju. Through so doing it provides practical examples that help develop an understanding of why cultural elements have become a significant factor in urban regeneration initiatives, and how cultural elements contribute to regenerative processes. On top of this, this book identifies three requirements for an area to be selected (Jungang-dong, Naedeok-dong and Suamgol in Cheongju) - to recognise the practical, cultural impacts on social regeneration. To identify the cultural contribution to the community, an area had to suffer from struggling urban deprivation symptoms (e.g. depopulation, building or house deterioration, or a decrease in the numbers of local business). Also, in order to gain a realistic opinion in the aspect of culture-led urban regeneration, people who directly observed the changing local environment where needed, and different local characteristics (e.g. location, the varied opportunities of cultural activities, and population distribution) were a necessary component to compare and understand the impacts of CCEA. The main purpose of this chapter is to explain the context of Cheongju city and three targeted areas

5.1. The City of Cheongju

Cheongju is an inland city located 128km away from South Korea's capital, Seoul. It is the capital and largest city of North Chungcheong Province (hereafter, Chungbuk). The city is not only the seat of the provincial government of Chungbuk, but it is also an important regional city with regards to economics, education and culture. As the most rapidly growing city in South Korea, the urban population of Cheongju has increased from 92,342 in 1960 to 630,637 in 2006 and was recorded as 841,219 in 2015. Furthermore, it is conveniently accessible from other areas via two motorways. It is also the case that the large size of its industrial complexes (Ochang Science Industrial

Complex and Osong Health Science Complex), and its four universities have resulted in further inward migration to the area.

Cheongju's economy has been transformed from being largely agriculture and manufacturing-based to being service-based over the last thirty years. According to the Quarterly Statistic Report of 2014, there are 56,243 businesses in total in Cheongju, made up of: wholesale and retail: 14,576 (24.3%), accommodation and food: 10,953 (19.5%), institutions, repair and individual businesses: 6,637 (11.8%), transportation: 5,218 (9.3%), manufacturing: 4,369 (7.8%). In addition, Cheongju is seeking to establish high-tech industries covering electricity, information and communication, biotechnology, mechatronics, aircraft, and transport industries to boost sustainable urban development, economic development, job creation and encourage population growth.

The radical economic change within the city region has been associated with several issues. Cheongju was ranked 17th amongst 84 areas in terms of city-wide deprivation in 2015. . Cheongju is reported to have had the highest deterioration in industrial structure, possess considerable health inequalities and insufficient medical facilities. In light of its industrial structure, the number of jobs in manufacturing has declined, and the financial self-sufficiency of the city is relatively low.

With regard to social change, Cheongju has not been immune from the pressures that South Korea has, nationally, faced with regards to having an ageing population, as well as low fertility and youth unemployment issues, In term of youth unemployment, the Chungbuk areas including Cheongju were ranked second in South Korea (the unemployment rate reached 5.4% in September 2014). Young people living in Cheongju are struck with lower-paid, temporary contracts and are the first to be laid off during crisis times. There is a continuous shortage of youth employment which has led to problems and threatened social harmony. In addition, it is estimated that Chungbuk's ageing population, which was 220,000 in 2014, will increase to 35.9% in 2040. The percentage of the population in Cheongju that is ageing is more rapid than in other cities. The proportion of people aged 65 was 6.2% in 2006 but reached 10.2% in 2014 (Newsis, 2014). According to the 2015 Official Social Survey, many of the elderly in Cheongju suffered from financial problems (48.8%), loneliness (28.8%), and health problems (10.4%) (Lee, 2016).

Social issues within the area can emerge in different ways. For instance, the population of Cheongju has increased since the city was integrated, but formerly the Cheongwon[1] area had suffered from an imbalance between developments within the city centre and surrounding suburban areas. It NIMBYism was generated in the former Cheongwon area, because the area had historically been targeted for more 'unwelcome' - development projects, such as landfill sites, incineration plants and other disposal facilities. The concentrated improvement and investment projects within the city centre created social exclusion, economic inequality and physical imbalances in the former Cheongwon area (See Appendix 2 for more information regarding Cheongju's circumstance – as evaluated using SWOT analysis).

5.2. Three Targeted Areas and Its Regenerative Urban Planning: Jungang-dong, Naedeok-dong and Suamgol

• Jungang-dong

Jungang-dong was the epicentre of business and commercial activities in central Cheongju until the late 1980s. However, due to growing developments within surrounding suburbs, coupled with the displacement of the neighbourhood's main facilities, the commercial competitiveness of Jungang started to decrease in the 1990s. Several commercial shops closed, and areas that had been economically buoyant started to experience a decline. The area has suffered from a decreasing population, increasing numbers of vacant shops, a reduction in population movement and 'slumification'. The depopulation of the area is a stark contrast to the overall population of Cheongju, which experienced a 35% rise between 1990 and 2013. Jungang district, which has experienced the fastest deterioration, has turned into a slum. Plummeting land values, the closing of shops and continuing deterioration processes have been identified as the prominent problems of the region.

In terms of regenerative urban planning, Jungang dong has experienced a 23.2% decline in commerce in the last 10 years (2004-2014). This has further fuelled urban deterioration. Some 79% of the buildings are aged 20 years or more, and as a result, the remodelling of empty buildings is imminent (An, 2015). Retail, commercial and cultural sectors are largely found within this area,

---

[1] Cheongwon: As Figure 5-1 demonstrates, originally Cheongju and Cheongwon were one city, but the government reformed the administrative divisions of the town cities afterKorean independence in 1945. The area of Cheongwon is actually 5 times bigger than Cheongju, whereas Cheongju's population is 4.5 times higher than Cheongwon. The debate regarding administrative integration has intensified since 2009. In 2012 a new city region being named Cheongju was created; a high-technology city which was envisaged to enhance regional competitiveness, promote linkages between urban and rural areas, and encourage economic activities.

but strategic maintenance and development have been stagnant because of the heavy focus on new land development. To prevent further deterioration, there have been various endeavours launched since 2001. Between 2005 and 2009, the Jungang Urban Regeneration Committee (hereafter, JURC) received funding from Cheongju City Council to create a car-free zone through a 450m pine tree-lined street within the centre of the market area. The project sought to revitalise the street and create a culturally vibrant street that was amenable to local businesses.

Along with the car-free zone project, a derelict theatre was replaced with an outdoor cultural zone for multiple purposes. This, it was hoped, would revitalise local businesses through cultural investment. In total, both projects cost $14 billion, which was funded by Cheongju Council. As a result, a wide range of cultural programmes emerged, from flea markets, craft exhibition spaces and regular music performance to small community-based festivals.

As the regeneration scheme was actively reflected upon, the Cheongju Urban Regeneration Trust Centre (hereafter, CURTC) was established and managed by local residents and academic experts. It received funding worth $44 million money to encourage the planning, management and implementation of the JURC in 2011. This acts as the headquarters for the JURC. The centre is funded and supported by resident organisations and the Cheongju City Council, and normally occupies a formerly vacant store or unoccupied buildings within the centre. Specifically, the CURTC has entrusted five vacant buildings for use as a social enterprise, leisure facilities and public offices. Distinctively, with support coming from the City Council, the buildings are operated by local residents who financially contributed to deposit, rental fees and refurbishment price. These regeneration efforts have attracted increasing visitors, as well as the growth of the local economy and internal investment.

- Naedeok-dong

Naedeok-dong is located to the north of Cheongju city and was well-known as a residential area until the late of 1980s. Its biggest Tobacco Factory was opened in 1946 and at its most successful produced 10 billion cigarettes each year with 3,000 workers. However, as a result of a decrease in consumption and increasing mechanisation, the factory was closed in 2004. After this, urban decline gradually set in within surrounding residential areas. Several neighbourhoods have vigorously complained about the derelict factory because the eyesore building triggered crime and juvenile delinquency. The area is also known for its high proportion of elderly households, and there have been several vacant stores and buildings which have suffered from decay. As a result, Naedeok-dong was designated as the fastest declining area in Cheongju in 2015. To overcome the deprivation, the Tobacco Factory was targeted for revival as a cultural complex as part of an economic-led urban regeneration initiative that was implemented since 2014. To fulfil the regeneration purpose, a number of notable strategies were such as encouraging culture and knowledge industries; creating a cultural business park through widening urban leisure facilities; enhancing greater diversity; and rebranding the area to attract visitors. Apart from injecting cultural elements, there was an attempt to revitalise the derelict areas by building high-quality office complexes, business centres, hotel developments, and leisure and entertainment facilities.

The flagship regeneration project was promoted by a wide range of financial structures. The Cheongju City Council, Korea Housing and Urban Guarantee Corporation (HUG), and private companies established the Real Estate Investment Trusts (REITs) to promote the project with \$171billion. In addition, \$45million from national and local government budgets were invested in cultural facilities and a road extension around the Tobacco Factory. However, the economic-led regeneration scheme has drawn criticism from the local authority. The Citizens' Coalition for Economic Justice Group (CCEJ) of Cheongju condemned the project for trying to concede too much to large capital circulation. The group insisted that as the project focuses on large private investment, the core purpose of the scheme, such as improving local residents' and local business' economic circumstances has been neglected.

- Suamgol

Suamgol village was formed by refugees from the Korean war who built unauthorised houses and settled down in the hillside. Between 1949 and 1955, the population of the village was around 64,000 to 81,000, but recently only 306 elderly (all over sixty) lives here in 2014. The village has poor access from the city centre, skills shortages due to the high elderly population, and poor environmental quality. In Significant deprivation has existed in the area for several decades, and the village has been named as the last shanty village in Cheongju.

In order to tackle the deprivation within the village, a public art-led regeneration project has taken place since 2008. It has employed artists and 10 students of a drawing department of the nearby university. Through the project, cultural and artistic popularity was given to Suamgol village. Its rising artistic reputation attracted the attention of a filmmaker, and as a result, the village was used as a drama location ('King of 164 Baking, Kim Takgu) in 2009. This spread the attractiveness of the villages to tourists from Japan, China, and Thailand. To maintain the positive phenomenon, 15 local residents have opened local businesses, called 'Masil', to improve the local economy through selling Suamgol souvenirs and local foods to visitors since 2011.

In 2013, artists created the 'Suamgol Arts Village' by using the vacant houses to provide cultural opportunities such as folk painting, water-colouring, pottery, and glassworks. To encourage the development of Suamgol, the Cheongju City Council and the Provincial Government of Chungcheongbuk-do support the costs of mural painting repairs, the management of the tourist information centre, and the building of public toilets and parking spaces. However, as the popularity of the village has grown, the proliferation of chain stores that have opened has frightened residents. Obvious gentrification has emerged through the building of chain stores, cafes, restaurants, and shopping centres around the village. Although Suamgol has been transformed by the arrival of artists and their creative efforts, such an invasion can generate the destruction of neighbourhood authenticity and result in the displacement of poor residents.

5.3. Introducing the Cultural City of East Asia Event

- Purposes of the CCEA

The primary aim of the CCEA was to share a mutual understanding of culture and strengthen a sense of unity by exchanging cultural activities in the region (refer to Section 1.4). It was recognised that, as cultural events have played a fundamental role in developing European cities, the CCEA could act as a powerful instrument to promote regional regeneration within East Asia (Myeongsung Park, the art director of CCEA). As a result, 'exchange cultural programmes', 'development and regeneration of provincial cities through cultural programmes', and 'building solidarity in the East Asia region' became the essential priorities of the event (City of Yokohama News Release, 2014).

- The Previous Experience of CCEA in Gwangju 2014

Gwangju, located in the Southwest corner of South Korea, was inaugurally chosen as the host location of the 2014 CCEA, along with Quanzhou in China and Yokohama in Japan. During this CCEA, Gwangju held more than 20 big cultural programmes, such as the World Music Festival, Gwangju Biennale, Gwangju World Arirang Festival, 2014 Asia Culture Forum, as well as partnership cultural events with central governments and local governments, and cultural workshops across the city for one year. After this, the first CCEA was evaluated, and it was argued that the cross-country nature of the events, and the range of public and private partners, not only helped to tackle conflicts between the three nations but also encouraged social development (Yokohama Joint Statement, 2014). Based on these positive results, the three nations announced the Yokohama Joint Statement in November 2014, which sought to establish continuous cooperation within the cultural sphere. The Statement includes declarations that the three provincial cities would:

I.   Further develop administration, culture, arts, tourism, economy and trade under the principle of reciprocity

II. Cooperate to allow for effective exchange between culture, arts organisations, businesses and citizens

III. Share the influential experience and encourage co-operation between businesses for enhancing cultural cities of East Asia

IV. Maintain an intimate and sustainable relationship between the related government agencies of the three nations, and frequently work together on issues of mutual interest (Pre-2014 Asia Culture Forum, 2014).

Lee, who was in charge of the cultural exchange with China and event management, spoke of the beneficial social and economic aspects that emerged during the 2014 CCEA:

"The CCEA led to rising job creation in the cultural and leisure economy sectors and increased the demanding of human labour force and businesses connected with the event. Particularly, the CCEA brought a positive perception that the national event could be hosted in metropolitan cities. It encouraged people's self-esteem for Gwangju city. In general, several large-sized cultural events in South Korea are often one-off, so criticisms are always voiced that there is nothing left after the end of the event. In this regard, the CCEA was an opportunity to create long-term cultural programmes and to regenerate the disadvantaged areas by using diverse cultural resources for a long time".

Using this as evidence of the success of the scheme, in 2015 Cheongju was able to expand and improve the hosting of the event.

- The CCEA in Cheongju – Programmes, Management, Structure and Specific Processes

[Origins]

Cheongju has long been renowned as a cultural and educational city, and its cultural resources epitomise the city's vibrancy and positively influences the lives of its citizens. The status of CCEA in 2015 reflected Cheongju's aspiration to drive forward both economically and culturally and offered a chance for residents to be proud of their history while celebrating the city's cultural diversity. In 2014, the judges admired Cheongju's great cultural heritage and praised the outstanding plans for 2015's CCEA, along with Qingdao of China and Nigata of Japan. The year-long series of programmes demonstrated cultural diversity from high art and international biennale to free music concerts. Furthermore, Cheongju sought to use the CCEA to transform the city from being primarily associated with an industrial base into a vibrant cultural city such as those found in Glasgow and Liverpool (Nam, 2015).

> "As the CCEA benchmarks the ECOC, the event would enhance the cultural exchange and forge a firm network with participated cities. Furthermore, the CCEA would make a constant effort in creating a sustainable cultural project in conjunction with the ECOC programmes" (CCEA website, 2015a).

[Management]

The policy to bid for the CCEA was first set up at the fourth culture Ministers' Meeting of South Korea-China-Japan in May 2012 in Shanghai, China (this is now known as the 'Shanghai' Action Plan). During this meeting, ministers from each country agreed to designate cultural cities for one year and encourage cultural exchange policies between the three nations (Gwangju Activity Report, 2015). The policy strategy was created under the premise of 'the integration of cultural exchange', 'consciousness of East Asia', and 'understanding of cultural partners'. Furthermore, as the event benchmarked the ECOC, the initiative aimed to prove the positive ripple effects about the contribution of culture in urban regeneration.

In terms of selecting the cities and the eligibility requirements, the size of a city did not matter with regard to whether it could become a CCEA host city, but it was acknowledged that there should be a balance between capital and provincial cities. Interested cities were required to enter a competition to stage the CCEA to confirm their cultural position in a league of East Asian cities. As a year-long scheme, a selected provincial city needed to be able to offer a wide range of cultural programmes, including partnership events in conjunction with the Ministry of Culture and Tourism; coordination of national cultural events; and the sharing of cultural exchange programmes between the arts, tourism and sports spheres. For the entire process of CCEA, the selected cities of three nations could receive funding from their local governments. In the case of Cheongju, $1.2billion in total was funded by the central, regional and local level governments of South Korea.

[Structure]

After Cheongju was awarded the bid, the CCEA Cheongju Office was set up in December 2014 as a non-profit organisation at the Cheongju Cultural Industry Promotion Foundation in Naedeok-dong. The office was in operation throughout the CCEA (from December 2014 to December 2015) and had a team of eight people. A number of these people were co-opted from government departments and private companies. The office was in charge of the organisation of cultural programming, events' delivery, the development of volunteers' programme, international relations around the CCEA, close communication with China and Japan, commercial activities from marketing, merchandising, communications, programme funding, and monitoring, and administration.

To help deliver the strategy and guide the overall processes of the CCEA, cultural expert O-Young Lee (former Minister of the Ministry of Culture, Sports and Tourism,) was co-opted as a chairman. He counselled the principal direction of xxx in relation to the opening and ending of performances, academic events, and other cultural programmes (Chungbuk in News, 2014). O-Young Lee provided expertise and offered a cultural and creative vision to the CCEA and Cheongju's development. In addition, the Committee for the CCEA at the local government level consisted of 21 members (in 2014) and represented a wide range of fields including the governments, universities, the Chungbuk art council, art institutions such as museums and the expo, and tourism organisations. In addition, 26 citizen members (such as members of Parliament, professors, academic researchers, the director of a broadcasting company, charity companies and community representatives) were selected to promote and encourage the CCEA. These Committees were mainly focused on the brand dimensions of the co-operative programmes, the economic impacts of the events, and any wider structural urban development effects that arose through the CCEA. In addition, they provided cross-sectoral consultation in terms of policy and the direction of cultural programmes.

[How Were Choices Made?]

For achieving the title of CCEA, the process required an explicit framework to be created. This required the winning city to demonstrate its capacities not only in providing existing and historical cultural strengths but also concerning creating sophisticated cultural programmes over the coming years. During the bidding process for the CCEA in 2014, Cheongju was acknowledged for its constant cultural efforts and development. Its physical infrastructure (e.g. cultural venues and accommodation capacities) were described as plentiful, and the city was praised for being not only prepared for the bidding, but also for holding the event itself. When evaluating the city's cultural attempts to boost urban development, the long-term social, economic and cultural impacts that were planned and evaluated were praised. In terms of the range and diversity of the cultural activities, it possessed the capacity to combine local cultural heritage and existing art forms with innovating and experimental cultural expressions in the city. The committee decided that there were abundant cultural offerings that were sufficient for the city to hold the title of

CCEA 2015. To win the bid, Cheongju had to meet four main criteria: 'the ability as the cultural city', 'the creation of constructive partnerships', 'a business plan', and 'a marketing strategy'. These four criteria – and how Cheongju met them, are explored in turn.

Table 5-1. Four main criteria for gaining the title of CCEA

---

1. Demonstrate Abilities as a Cultural City

The city must provide a strong commitment to the development of cultural sectors, while also possessing vibrant strategies to boost a city through cultural programmes. To meet this requirement, Cheongju demonstrated:
  - ➢ A medium and long-term plan to further develop a cultural policy and identify the previous achievement of cultural policies
  - ➢ A plan for urban development and regeneration through the cultural city strategy, and to demonstrate a prior commitment to regional development by integrating cultural programmes within wider city strategies.
  - ➢ A specific plan for hosting the international cultural event and a cultural exchange strategy

2. Creation of Constructive Partnerships

The city must demonstrate its ability to create partnership arrangements, including details on committee composition and the establishment of a secretariat as a central feature in leading to successful cultural and urban development. It was also important to demonstrate effective partnership working to promote and implement cultural event strategies. Cheongju demonstrated its strength in these areas via the well-organised composition of its committee and executive officers. In addition, bilateral partnerships between central government, private partners and third sectors such as local enterprise, universities, arts institutions were a key characteristic of the strategy.

3. Business Plans

Creating an effective business plan for the full year was a fundamental step to increase the efficiency of the project. Cheongju included the following plans in its proposal.
  - ➢ A clear and concise business plan with explanations of specific practices, to avoid unrealistically high expectations
  - ➢ The desire for sustainability by applying creative and resident-focused cultural programmes
  - ➢ The engagement of experts from various fields of urban planning, including representatives from universities, local companies, art organisations and community groups.

> ➢ The feasibility of businesses in exchanging cultural programmes between the three nations.
> ➢ A strategy for contributing to urban development and regeneration through a cultural approach
> ➢ Propriety of funding and the ability to deliver CCEA projects

4. Marketing Strategy

One more important requirement for the bid was the marketing strategy. Cheongju emphasised its ability to foster diversity, encourage culture-led activities, create high-quality programming of events to bring more visitors and tourists, as well as its ability to create easily accessible programmes for all people, re-branding the city through cultural activities, and allowing an effective usage of local facilities. Also, Cheongju provided a strategy for the securing budget, a plan to attract local residents' participation and a long-term plan once the CCEA is introduced.

[Programmes]

Some 100,000 visitors attended the programmes throughout the year and, once the CCEA was finished, it was considered to have been the best cultural project since Cheongju city was created. The programmes were divided into two sections – partnership events and special events. Partnership events covered most of the cultural programmes that operated during the CCEA, and special events generally described the academic forums, workshops and partnership businesses. According to newspapers and local leaflets, 27 primary events were undertaken during the year. The listed events (See Appendix 3) lasted for at least three days, and the full CCEA programmes included not only full events but also overall exhibition days, performance days, and educational classes, bringing the total number of events to 70. Most activities were directly procured by the government, the Cheongju Art Council, and small arts and community organisations. Through organising CCEA programmes, the cultural fields of Cheongju formed extensive partnerships across public, private and third sectors. Cheongju has considered culture as being central to its urban regeneration agenda for many years, and the CCEA and related programmes were viewed as adding significant added value to existing regeneration programmes:

"Our creative culture-led regeneration scheme at the former Tobacco Factory and diverse range of cultural opportunities from the international biennale to small performances led to successfully have the title of CCEA. And such the national event would magnify the significance for further Cheongju's cultural approach regeneration projects" (Lee, Mayor of Cheongju, interviewed in Jungbu Daily, 2014).

The scale of the impacts that emerged throughout 2015 encouraged Cheongju's existing culture-led urban regeneration scheme and allowed the results to be more solid and substantial.

The CCEA programmes tended to operate on multiple levels, particularly with regard to cultural exchange, city promotion, and urban regeneration. Several issues should be addressed with regard to this. First, cultural exchange activities were co-ordinated by the three nations' CCEA committee, and traditional cultural performances were hosted in each nation which also involved a culture swap of young people (e.g. to experience different cultures and lifestyles). Second, Cheongju adapted various partnership events and linked with the government to widely promote the city as a culturally vibrant area. Third, and to create a sustainable urban regeneration environment, the CCEA programmes encouraged residents' participation in various cultural activities such as volunteering, community contests, donation of their own cultural works, art classes, and performances. When it comes to culture-led regeneration, the engagement of local residents is a crucial factor in creating a successful project. In this sense, a wide range of cultural offerings for all residents during the CCEA raised awareness of culture-led regeneration. Furthermore, a range of more tangible outcomes through residents' positive contributions to the event, promoting the rehabilitation of Cheongju's image, and community cooperation increased not only residents' knowledge of Cheongju's culture and heritage, but also the importance of cultural participation within regeneration.

5.4. The Strengths and Limitations of the CCEA as a Regeneration Project

By hosting the second CCEA in 2015, Cheongju city received unprecedented national recognition as a city of culture and was given an opportunity to bring out its innovative cultural ideas, the enthusiasm of people, and creative skills. Furthermore, arts and culture offered a bigger stage to further urban regeneration initiatives. During the CCEA, the abundant cultural programmes and events proved capable of producing noticeable effects in the host city. In this section, I explore what happened during the CCEA and examine its influence on the regeneration schemes.

- Economic Impacts of the CCEA

An evaluation of the economic benefits of the 2015 CCEA has not officially been revealed; however, some individual projects have published data on the direct and indirect economic benefits of their events. In this section, I discuss the benefits of the Cheongju International Craft Biennale, the Cheongwon Organic Life Festival, Cheongju Fortress Festival, and the King Sejong and Chojeong Water Festival, which were the main big events during the CCEA.

I. The 9th Cheongju International Craft Biennale (16th Sep ~ 25th Oct 2015)

The number of tourists to the Biennale rose slightly, up to more than 314,021, including 15,700 foreign visitors when compared to 300,300 tourists in 2013. It seems there was a small increase in attendance between 2013 and 2015. The biennale sparked interest from visitors and artists, despite the deadly outbreak of Middle East Respiratory Syndrome (MERS) and a significant economic slump in 2015 (Kim, 2015a). During the Biennale, 2000 artists came from 45 nations and more than 7,500 artworks were exhibited. The programmes included a 'special exhibition of Alain de Botton', a 'Kids biennale', 'pre-docent education in the biennale venues', 'Cheongju International craft and art fairs', 'street markets', 'International craft academic conference', and 'traditional craft workshops', which all added value to the CCEA development. Particularly, the art fair ($330m), the craft fair ($240m), and the street market ($57m) generated some $630m in revenue (by 24th October 2015) within the craft sector. This sum was 60% greater than the sum recorded in 2013 ($400m). Furthermore, the biennale provided an opportunity for xxx to reach out and to establish a world craft cluster in Cheongju.

II. Cheongwon Organic Life Festival (2nd Oct ~ 11st Oct 2015)

The festival began to promote the agricultural products of Cheongju in 2008 (Choi, 2016). According to the 2015 visitor report of the Cultural Contents Research Centre at the University of Chungcheong, 480,000 tourists visited the festival, an increase compared to 2011 (total visitors were 200,000). There was notable growth in tourist numbers during the CCEA. The festival sold various organic agricultural products at between 10% and 30% cheaper than standard market prices (Han, 2016). During the festival in 2015, these products generated $350m in revenue while helping to support local agricultural merchants.

III: The 10th King Sejong & Chojeong Mineral Spring Water Festival (27th May ~ 29th May 2015)

During the festival, there were 65,710 visitors to Cheongju, which was a slight rise on the previous year. 48% of the total visitors were foreign visitors. These visits generated an economic impact of $162.6 million (Ahn, 2016)

- Social Impacts

The CCEA generated many social impacts through various cultural programmes. As mentioned above, culture-led urban regeneration was one of the imperative purposes of 2015 CCEA, so the event included several resident-led cultural programmes for recognising the importance of urban regeneration. These included the improvements made to social cohesion through voluntary works, community solidarity, providing cultural education for young people, and accepting different cultures. In particular, the Cheongju International Craft Biennale set overarching goals for resident engagement. For example, 27,912 people, including Cheongju citizens, schools, and community organisations, voluntarily participated in collecting unused CDs, and broadcast them outside the main venues; they contained messages of hope. This co-operative artwork programme created various development community networks, as well as strengthening community solidarity, helping people feel a sense of belonging, and increased senses of self-worth. For developing citizen involvement in the cultural sector, the CCEA sought to resident-led programmes such as an exhibition of participants' belongings, local resident-led concert, volunteering in the promotion of the cultural project, and translating works in English, Chinese and Japanese (Kim, 2015b). One volunteer said that "the arts and culture were a delight and offered enjoyment that I have never felt, and the cultural participation also helped me to take up a career within the cultural field".

Throughout a year-long period, various local-based programmes encouraged participation from a wide range of groups including civic clubs, youth groups and local artistic communities. This helped not only enhance citizen awareness of Cheongju's cultural competitiveness but also strengthened cultural solidarity amongst residents and offered them a degree of pride in their locality (Yoo, 2016).

Furthermore, the CCEA paid significant attention to the exchange of young people between the three nations. Selected students from each country were offered a number of different experiences, such as participation in traditional cultural activities and home-stay experiences with native people. The young people of the three nations were offered a tour of Cheongju's traditional market, Korean paper 'Hanji' making, chopstick making, and Korean folk painting in Cheongju. One participant from Japan noted how participants could learn co-operative harmony through cultural activities which involved working with friends. Another student from China also praised the project on the basis that all the activities were enjoyable and impressive, and further noted how the most meaningful thing during the exchange programme was the ability to make friends from different countries. This experience provided not only cultural knowledge and diversity but also helped to improve social and language skills. Such cultural exchange programmes for young people during the CCEA helped to expand cultural opportunities and acted as an investment in the cultural education of the next generation.

- The Impact of a City's Image

Cultural projects can play a crucial role in celebrating local cultures and positively changing a city's image (Matarasso, 1997). As the CCEA programmes aimed to promote cities involved, the event significantly contributed to branding the Cheongju as a cultural city (Seunghoon Lee, Mayor of Cheongju, 2016). Mayor Seunghoon Lee emphasised that the success of the CCEA was that it illustrated the history and culture of a thousand years with modern values. It helped to frame the city as one where traditional and modern cultures operated harmoniously. Furthermore, the status of the city has been firmly solidified as a cultural city; generating an adaptable cultural environment with a secured budget for cultural businesses. Some residents positively responded to the image change from a typical industrial city into a lively cultural city.

The city received considerable media coverage. During the CCEA, there was an immediate increase in media attention focused on Cheongju; as shown in Figure 5-1. Cheongju was mentioned seven times more in the media than in 2014, while the media paid more attention to Cheongju's cultural issues after the completion of the CCEA than in 2014 (229 coverage in 2014. 1,689 in 2015, and 593 in 2016). It is also worthy of note that the coverage continued well after the completion of the event in 2016.

Figure 5-1: Media coverage during the CCEA

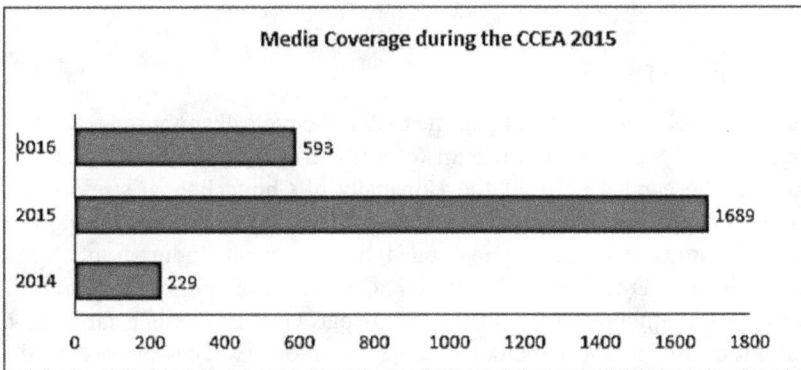

Source: NAVER (A representative internet content service operator in South Korea [Counted by author]

- The Increased Value of Culture Through the CCEA

The year-long cultural event also brought various benefits in terms of culture. The event created an environment in which the public benefitted from a wealth of diverse cultures. Through the various cultural programs and exchange activities of the CCEA, there were expansions in the associations that existed with other local governments and numerous cultural organisations (Ministry of Culture, Sports and Tourism, 2015). Cheongju's effort in promoting culture led to a 47% increase in art and cultural grants from central government. This funding has been invested in stimulating art and culture; developing cultural programmes and making Cheongju a key town in its region (Ahn, 2016).

Another positive impact of CCEA was that by highlighting the hidden cultural themes such as Jikji, the history of King Sejong, and Myeongsim Bogam[2], the CCEA helped to increase residents' cultural awareness and an appreciation of the region's diverse history. Additionally, the cultural effects spread out to Cheongju's other existing industries such as agriculture, biotechnology, and even the beauty industry. Altogether, it has helped form a positive impression for the future; that Cheongju has abundant and diverse commercial themes as well as enhanced cultural elements (Byun, 2015).

The most important benefit from the CCEA is that Cheongju established solid cultural networks with cultural cities in China and Japan. Practically, the Cheongju Culture Industry Foundation has planned to take several cultural projects to other CCEA-hosted cities (e.g. 2014: Gwangju, Quanzhou, Yokohama / 2015: Qingdao, Niigata / 2016: Jeju Special Self-Governing Province, Ningbo, Narasi) over subsequent years. The 2015 CCEA became a keystone in establishing a global cultural environment (Lee, Mayor of Cheongju, 2016). The CCEA also brought investment for a further cultural city project from 2016 with $3.4 million in funding from the central and regional governments.

- Limitations of the CCEA

During the roll-out and hosting of the CCEA, the typically imposed top-down approach still practised within South Korea was criticised. Lee, Head of Cultural Contents Research Centre at the University of Chungcheong, stressed the importance of creating the right structures during the forum for the Chung-buk cultural industry in 2016. He said that the event industry of North Chungcheong Province had created chronic problems; local cultural businesses frequently faced difficulties in participating in such large-sized cultural events, as the structure of the event industry relies heavily on the bidding of public organisations rather companies or consumers bidding. In line with this, cultural enterprises at a local level had few opportunities during the CCEA. There were attractive cultural events held during the CCEA such as the chopstick festival, the international craft biennale, the organic industry expo, and so on. However, the rate of local business participation was only

---

[2] Myeongsim Bogam: It is an ancient Chinese book containing a collection of aphorisms and quotations from the Chinese classics and other works.

8.6%, while businesses from elsewhere accounted for 91.3% of participants. As a result, it could be concluded that local business received just around $1.5 million, with around $16 million being directed elsewhere. Increasing contracts with big companies or businesses from other regions resulted in an outflow of funds and meant that the event had a limited positive on the local economy. Indeed, it facilitated the tardy development of local events.

Chapter 6

The Impacts of Culture and Arts on Social Regeneration: Community Development and Living Circumstance

This book takes as its starting point debates on cultural activities and seeks to understand the interrelationships between culture-led regeneration and social regeneration by looking at residents' views and opinions rather than measuring the economic or tourism impacts of xxx. Based on the purposes, this chapter asks 'have culture-led approaches created social regeneration opportunities in Cheongju and, if so, what opportunities and for whom?', 'what are the possible problems and tensions in using cultural events to support social regeneration in Cheongju?', and 'How does the CCEA in Cheongju reinforce or challenge wider literature on the role of cultural events in social regeneration?'. To answer these questions, 74 respondents (for details of respondents, see Appendix 1) participated in a questionnaire and in-depth interviews. Local residents were given top priority in this book to widen understanding as to how people evaluate cultural approaches to regeneration and the impact of the same on communities and individual environments. Therefore, most explanation within this chapter comes from local residents' opinions and their detailed feelings and attitudes towards cultural engagement and social regeneration aspects.

6.1 Residents' General Perceptions of Cultural Provision

In order to evaluate the significance of the cultural event – CCEA, the general perception of cultural provision in the city was discussed with respondents to understand how they consider culture and arts. Firstly, the positive opinions are founded as follows. Jungang-dong residents recognised, with regard to cultural perceptions, that local festivals help create frequent engagement with neighbours and families. Additionally, cultural resources play a leading role in developing the environment and communities. As large cultural institutions are located in Naedeok-dong, residents consider that the representative cultural institutions offer various cultural opportunities, from national events to family-centred programmes. As a result, they can enrich residents' daily routines. In the case of Suamgol, cultural works made this village colourful and implanted a positive cultural perception through a special mural painting project. Such artworks have the potential to bring significant popularity to the area.

By reviewing the answers, cultural perception is established by the degree of cultural experience and cultural projects. In Jungang-dong, the success of a car-free zone project, which was one culture-led urban regeneration initiative held between 2005 and 2009, contributed to a positive cultural perception in the area. Naedeok-dong respondents were influenced by several cultural opportunities at the Cheongju Culture Industry Promotion Foundation, and culture-based regenerative projects that helped revive the former Tobacco Factory. In addition, public arts-led regeneration schemes (e.g. mural painting) in 2007 had a significant influence on creating a positive cultural perception in Suamgol. Respondents of the three neighbourhoods highlighted their positive cultural experiences with the projects and discussed their growing perceptions of culture-related activities:

Table 6-1. Residents' opinions regarding cultural perception

[Jungang-dong]

"After completion of the car-free zone for urban regeneration, diverse cultural programmes started to come up on the newly paved road. For example, youth performances (dance, singing, playing), sports experiences, regular community festivals (Kimchi-making for the winter, busking performance), and historical exhibitions in the outdoor square (Japanese Military Sexual Slavery exhibition) were held over the three years. New and tidy environments, and the community-based programmes, created a positive cultural impression in my mind" (J-2).

"The plentiful cultural opportunities had the potential to revitalise Jungang-dong's market street again. Such cultural efforts seemed to be more of a driver in stimulating residents' engagement than before" (J-4).

[Naedeok-dong]

"I took part in a craft-making session during the International Craft Biennale in 2013, and family activities in 2014 at the CCIPF. Such cultural offerings played an enjoyable role in developing my life to make it more fun and vibrant" (N-3).

"I reckon that the cultural events taking place around Naedeok-dong has the capability to enhance local businesses. Naedeok-dong is one of the most deprived areas in Cheongju, and I feel that local business is now more at risk than ever before. During the event periods, however, cultural provisions (e.g.

---

advertisements or street performances) helped to brightly boost the local environment, and also provided a glimpse at the economic benefits of local business" (N-6).

[Suamgol]

"Participating in mural painting work with artists and residents were an unforgettable experience. Surely, cultural activity gave pride for the Suamgol community, and I have seen a significant change" (S-2 and S-4).

"Apart from the mural paintings, I enjoyed visiting the diverse exhibitions around Cheongju and other cities. When I first encountered such cultural life at, it felt a waste of money, and I did not know enough to enjoy some of the art events and was not comfortable at many of the arts events. However, trying to be engaged with the cultural environment has now helped me to recover my physical as well as mental health" (S-1).

Despite these positive perceptions, there was also a range of negative issues noted. Non-participants frequently said that 'financial problems' were the biggest barrier to participating in cultural events (33%). Three respondents mentioned that the reasons of financial difficulty and a lack of interest are both linked. It means that "I have been struggling with a lack of finance, which makes me indifferent to participating in cultural activities. Coming from a typical working-class background, there is not enough time, money and or a leisurely mind, although a number of programmes were spread out in Naedeok-dong" (N-4). "Arts and cultural activities are a luxury and quite a burden to ordinary residents living in our village. Attractive cultural programmes usually come with an unaffordable price" (S-3). "High price is always an obstacle. I surely agree that high quality and outstanding performance are worthy of a high price, but most qualified cultural programmes seem to be aimed at the higher-income groups and elites" (J-1).

Other reasons included the belief that venues are too far from their homes (21%), they have no interest in cultural participation (18%), they have very little information of cultural programmes (15%), and cultural programmes are unattractive to residents (13%). In discussing the indifference that can often be related to cultural participation, one respondent (N-5) insisted that "the average population of Naedeok-dong is aged between 50 and 70, and they are not familiar with getting involved in cultural activities as there has not been enough time to spend on their own leisure activity over the last 30 years". Instead, they have to focus on hard work and looking after their family. To them, cultural participation is not their business, and it is merely considered a waste of time and money. Another respondent (N-1) said, "I rarely hear about the cultural programmes in time, and I do not have enough cultural knowledge as well. These factors make me prefer to do other things in my spare time". In Suamgol, the indifference factor was connected to residents' old age. S-8 stated that as they get older, the elderly tend to stop engaging because of many reasons such as health, transport accessibility, finance and no one to go with. He concisely stated that these reasons generate "inevitable indifference" in Suamgol. Moreover, a lack of information and unattractive cultural offerings generate growing indifference in cultural activities.

It can be argued that the hosting of the events emphasised their own negative cultural perceptions, for example, by enforcing a belief that culture and arts programmes can interrupt local business and are a waste of money and time, can provoke a feeling of isolation for disabled people, that such events are only for the sake of an 'elite', that they are expensive, and create significant gentrification. These pessimistic perceptions were often influenced by respondents' backgrounds, interests and attitudes. The above noted cultural barriers tended to cause non-participants to stereotype or make generalisations about establishing their own cultural perceptions.

6.2. The Impacts of the CCEA:
Before the CCEA – The Impacts of Culture-led Projects on Social Regeneration

Before discussing the potential impacts of the CCEA, respondents were asked the question "do you think that cultural projects are a crucial driver to regenerate and develop a community and living environment?" This was designed to assess residents' opinions regarding how culture-led projects can influence social regeneration. As respondents were living in culture-led regeneration subjected areas, the residents had an authentic point of view and a sense of realism concerning the direct and indirect impacts of the CCEA. These results are informative and can help to identify the role of cultural projects in declining communities.

6.2.1. Have Cultural-led Projects and Regeneration Schemes Contributed to Community Development?

First, a question was asked as to whether previous culture-led projects had contributed to community development. As can be seen in Figure 6-1, different results appeared in different neighbourhoods.

Figure 6-1: Have cultural-led projects and regeneration schemes contributed to community development?

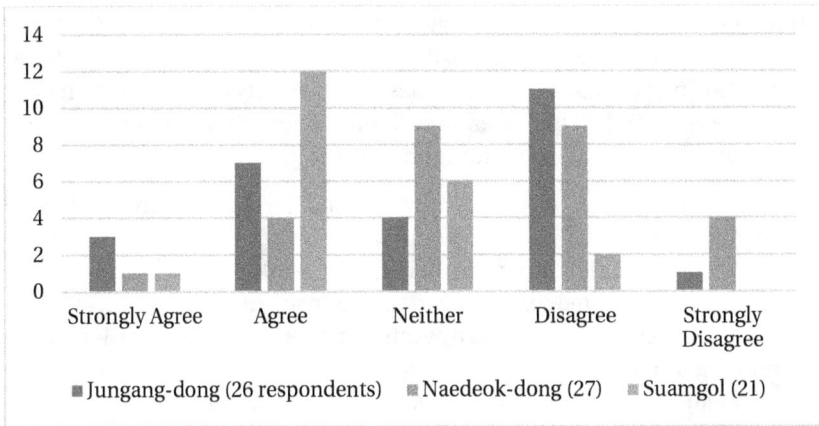

- Jungang-dong

For almost 15 years, Jungang-dong has held a number of different culture-led projects (such as the creation of a car-free zone) for urban regeneration to transform the community's image. Official newspapers published and highlighted the success of Jungnag-dong – the declined Jungang-dong area has become the active cultural place (Lee, 2016a), Jungang-dong has become the hot spot of successful culture-led urban regeneration (Lee, 2013), a number of local governments visited Jungang-dong to learn how to successfully mediate between public and communities (Shin, 2015). Thus, it can be argued that Jungang-dong has become an example of a successful culture-led regeneration area. A couple of respondents emphasised that by closing commercial shops and moving out core public facilities from the 1990s, the market street of Jungang-dong has become 'shadowed'. The merchant shops were reduced from more than 100 to around 40 between the late 1990s and the 2000s. However, after starting the car-free zone project and introducing several local festivals within the zone, the market street has metamorphosed with substantial cultural projects (J-5). In addition, the floating population has seemed to increase again, and the commercial district is slightly revived. It is believed that "Jungang-dong shows gradual development through the active cultural programmes on the street and in unused buildings" (J-4). In this sense, the mixture of culture and urban regeneration projects has transformed the arts and culture provision across Jungang-dong as well as Cheongju. It also has added value to the culture and locality since 2006 and played an incubator role in attracting residents' participation in the process of urban regeneration. In further, cooperating with local businesses that tend to be marginalised in the process of regeneration schemes would generate more positive long-term synergy in developing communities and creating employment.

However, the questionnaires also showed that 46% of respondents disagreed and strongly disagreed. In the main, they had sceptical views as to the cultural contribution of regeneration programmes to community development. In their view, there were no striking differences in the community's environment, and none of the changes was generated by culture-led projects.

> "Newspaper articles and civil servants tend to focus on the visible environment changes and announce the positive issues. Although cultural programmes provided benefits to Market Street and some residents, culture-led projects did not impact upon a minority of Jungang-dong residents for many years. I cannot see any positive legacy resulting from culture-led projects, either in Jungang-dong or the Cheongju city more generally" (J-6).

> "If culture and arts had intended to develop the community, the organisers or directors should have investigated what people and the community really need prior to undertaking culture-led regeneration initiatives or other culture-related projects. There is always media discussion about the growth of the local economy and the achievement of local government or a civil servant in relation to the cultural development of Jungang-dong as well as Cheongju, but the culture-led projects did not try to tackle any socio-economic problems of the community such as unemployment or the repair of housing" (J-3).

In terms of the working environment of the l community, a floating population was created which was increasingly made up of outsiders and citizens, and the commercial district has been gradually revived through cultural approaches to regeneration. However, the merchants of Market Street of Jungang-dong had different views. They insisted that there had been plentiful cultural activities around Market Street and that the area has become more energetic than before. However, it is not what it looks like from a merchant point of view. Although Jungang-dong benefited from the car-free zone project because it allowed the introduction of abundant cultural programmes, the project actually blocked car access and led to a decreasing number of consumers. Another key fact to remember is that loud noises generated from the cultural square seriously interrupt business, so there is sometimes furious hostility to cultural programmes. As a matter of fact, after creating a youth square in 2008 as part of the regeneration initiative, a few young people visited, even though there were no performances until early 2015 and the square is sometimes filled with rubbish. Such a situation is detrimental to the area's living and working environment. "The primary intention of cultural intervention was meaningful, but the actual management has weaknesses, and contribution to the community is left at zero" (J-6).

• Naedeok-dong

Despite Naedeok-dong being ranked as the most run-down area in Cheongju, it possesses an abundance of cultural elements, and the inaugural economic-led urban regeneration project has been in operation since 2014. Plentiful cultural opportunities played an important role in developing Naedeok-dong, and its vibrancy has also performed a crucial role in the decision-making process of the inaugural economic-led urban regeneration initiative. In the process of economic-led urban regeneration, the site of the former Tobacco Factory has been given new life by cultural injections. Along with the regeneration scheme, cultural facility expansion, the creation of a cultural street, and remodelling of the CCIPF were set up as cultural investment projects. These constant and abundant cultural efforts attracted broad investments, including the construction of the National Modern Gallery, developing cultural education, creation performing arts spaces, and enhancing the environment of the small street. Through this change, the surrounding environment became brighter. For example, the adjacent street – Andeokbul – is being developed. Several artistic sculptures, mural paintings and flower planting works have been introduced.

Additionally, the increasing cultural attempts could encourage more people to participate in cultural activities and enhance longer-term sustainability. Naedeok-dong sees culture and arts as part of a long-term growth strategy; therefore, a flourishing culture-led scene would help to make the area a destination for tourism as well as business investment. Conversely, there were also negative reactions that emerged in the questionnaire results. Almost 50% of survey participants said that they could not identify a positive cultural influence on community development. One of the respondents who volunteered at the 2013 International Craft Biennale insisted that the benefits of cultural involvement had often failed to reach the community.

"I voluntarily participated in promoting the 2013 International Craft Biennale. The volunteering offered a special opportunity to not only network with people but also to learn cultural knowledge. However, I am not sure whether the Biennale brought positive impacts to our community. The Biennale itself has a crucial possibility to attract people, received plenty of media attention, and attracted internal investment; however, I have not noticed that aid in generating thriving cultural projects for community development".

Several criticisms were focused on the current economic-led urban regeneration project. Many newspaper articles negatively reported on the regeneration scheme of Naedeok-dong, highlighting the rampant privatisation of the area, the failure to attract adequate investment, and the exclusion of residents' needs (Isak, 2015, and Yeonhap news, 2016). N-2 said such regeneration attempts stimulate more radical community demolition: "the economic-led urban regeneration scheme has the intention of demolishing the historical building to establish a cultural quarter. The Tobacco Factory is the cultural and symbolic asset of Naedeok-dong, but just tearing it down instead of preserving it is not the point of urban regeneration and threatens to break up the community. Unreasonable cultural injection would spoil local features and the environment". According to N-1 (a merchant who worked around the Tobacco Factory), currently, the area has been privatised and commercialised. The urban regeneration initiative provokes a large private company's franchise launch, and then the circumstances that led to the collapse of local businesses. In the same vein, N-5 insisted that "any attempts to change or transform the urban landscapes and buildings were complicated". However, none of the developers or stakeholders had specific awareness or background information about the targeted spaces. In addition, they never explained how to integrate the regenerative project with local businesses or how residents could use the places effectively. In this sense, culture-led projects create profits for developers and stakeholders, rather than improving the living or working environment of local residents.

- Suamgol

Suamgol experienced a transformation over 10 years. Questionnaire respondents (62%) were more likely to positively agree that culture-led projects had contributed to community improvement than those from Jungang-dong and Naedeok-dong. Within Suamgol, the iconic mural paintings have been constantly used as cultural motifs to attract cultural tourists and visitors. Distinctive integration between the shanty towns and the public artworks is still cited as a reason for tourists' visiting. Many residents had a positive attitude to the changes that had occurred through cultural and artistic works (mainly mural paintings) because this village had become vigorous and energetic through various cultural initiatives. Above all, the public art projects sought to regenerate the culturally and economically excluded village and resulted in amazing transformation (e.g. a hideous street was transformed into a galley). As a result, "Suamgol has been crowded with tourists, including drama fans from China, Japan and Thailand, and cultural visitors" (S-2). Cultural transformation was a key way to sustain the community, and it has become the motivation to advance future community strategies. For instance, the cultural popularity of Suamgol has led to the opening of new shops and community-owned businesses. The local shop 'Masil' was opened by local residents in 2011 to generate local economic benefits and create a local food business at a filming location. This not only created a binding force within Suamgol but also brought tourists and members of the community together.

However, due to its cultural popularity, gentrification has become a significant issue in Suamgol. The village has been thrown open by real estate agencies and developers, and this has damaged the village's authenticity and has threatened existing local shops. S-2 stressed that "attracting new investment is a good phenomenon to the community, and it means economic benefits are created in and around the village. However, the thoughtless construction for building a café, a franchised-restaurant and a shopping-mall can spoil the characteristics of Suamgol and impact residents' life. The disappearance of our tradition and local features make residents sorrowful. Becoming a gentrified area might badly affect the living environment, and the Suamgol, as well as villagers, would experience deprivation again".

Additionally, as a famous film location, enormous cultural investment has been poured into Korean drama and film-related projects (e.g. creation of drama street and drama theme park). Lastly, another concern related to the lack of privacy that could hamper the community's living environment. Some of the respondents strongly expressed their view that privacy is at risk of being invaded by those who visit to view Suamgol's artworks. As the artistic works dominate Suamgol, some visitors knock at the door asking to see the interior of the house and even took a photograph of the resident's laundry. Many residents stressed that privacy-related issues should be solved to make a more comfortable and sustainable community.

6.3. The CCEA Impacts on Social Regeneration: Influences on Community Development

When it comes to community development, there are various positive and negative points of view. In the case of Naedeok-dong, the level of positive responses was higher than in both Jungang-dong and Suamgol. As Naedeok-dong has the greatest extent of high levels of deprivation in Cheongju, the area tends to be unattractively identified to citizens, as well as visitors. However, the 2015 CCEA was a way to accelerate the area's image as culturally vibrant. During the CCEA, a number of community benefits were delivered by involving members of the community in Naedeok-dong. As an example, there was one event 'the Largest Display of Compact Discs' during the 2015 International Craft Biennale. Its purpose was to fill the dilapidated tobacco factory with donated old CDs, consisting of 489,440 from the community, schools, 11 different nations and 19 other cities.

In order to create the façade, many residents volunteered and took full ownership; by collecting and displaying the CDs. Reinvigorating the area brought community benefits in terms of making the area an attractive cultural destination. In addition, during the 2015 CCEA, there were diverse community and citizen group competition programmes in the fields of singing, dance, and performance. A participant in the citizen group competition expressed that "this opportunity gave us collective memory, experiences and a united mind. Building community solidarity is an essential step towards further community improvement".

In terms of the working environment, the potential growth of the local business economy was underlined as an impact of the big festivals that rippled throughout the local economy. For example, the usual customers of local shops are individuals, but sales to family units increased during the CCEA. In particular, the off-site cultural programmes of big festivals created revenue for businesses. In addition, the growth of the nightlife economy boosted revenue during the summer period. There were various night-programmes, including night art screenings and performances around the CCIPF. Due to the increase in visitors, many local businesses extended their opening times from 8 am – 8 pm to 8 am – 11 pm (N-8). "Such a wide variety of parade and street performances that worked to create a vibrant living environment" (N-1). It was emphasised that, in the past, many cultural activities were arranged inside the venue. However, as street performance and activities, which required active engagement from the public, took place outside, Naedeok-dong's atmosphere seemed more dramatic and enjoyable. Such an environment made residents more comfortable and safer, especially when walking at night.

Moreover, the area surrounding the Tobacco Factory, and other small streets in Naedeok-dong were improved. "The cultural atmosphere generated through the cultural events became a deterrent for crime and violence during the CCEA. In this sense, the CCEA was a vehicle to deter crime and fear and encourage a sense of community" (N-7).

On the other hand, some of the residents pointed out that the CCEA was not effectively adopted in Naedeok-dong. It was argued that it became a meretricious large-scale event that took place for the following reasons: city promotion, encouraging cultural consumption, and generating benefits to specified people or organisations. A resident emphasised that if the event wanted to provide leverage for community development, it needed to create community values. However, the event did not consider any characteristics of the local community, for instance, sharing information across communities and using local stories. Due to the lack of engagement with the community, it failed to draw in genuine local residents who were not interested in cultural programmes. "Just showing off the mega-event did not encourage actual participation within the community. The event should have identified the key features and a clear sense of place ahead of hosting the event".

Secondly, hosting the CCEA in Cheongju had great potential to contribute to the growth of Jungang-dong. In 2015, Cheongju received a lot of media attention due to the CCEA, and it helped to promote Jungang-dong's culture-led urban regeneration project. This could attract the interest of investors and organisations and positively contribute to the growth of the local economy and community enhancement (J-7). Moreover, an increase in cultural investment and an influx of tourists would be helpful to develop the area's working environment, particularly around the market street (J-4).

Although the reputation of Cheongju has been widely disseminated by hosting the CCEA, local residents are still sceptical. They insisted that the CCEA stimulates thinking about 'whose culture' is addressed in the process of a mega-event. There was little in the CCEA for ordinary people. People were unable to find out the possible CCEA impacts upon community development. Particularly, the merchants who were the non-CCEA participants were more dubious as to the relationship between hosting the CCEA and its ability to create a better working and living environment. "Although the big-event takes place at a certain period, the benefits seem flowing to the political elites and organisers. Any practical benefits to ordinary residents or the small local shops were not noticed. The CCEA was the largest cultural event ever before in Cheongju, but CCEA itself was not the way to change working or living environment over the short term" (J-6 and J-9).

Thirdly, many cultural programmes took place in Suamgol. As a majority of residents are elderly, they could easily get involved. In this sense, people's positive feelings were affected by the event. S-1 said, "the event was helpful to revitalise the community environment, and such excitement just does not end up in a day, the feeling maintains for a long time". However, some of the residents noted that Suamgol already had varied cultural programmes, including glass crafts, mural paintings, watercolour painting. They, therefore, had a negative perception because nothing changed during the CCEA, and the same cultural opportunities were offered to visitors and residents.

"There were also several concerns with regards to issues pertaining to the living environment of Suamgol. One resident who had managed a local shop for more than 40 years mentioned that the large size event had certainly contributed to the growth of the local economy. However, to improve the living environment, it was also important to repair the deterioration of the built environment and widen the street for more parking spaces. Although plentiful cultural projects were in progress in Suamgol, residents did not feel at ease from the threat of crime and their living circumstances, broken pavements and vacant lots remain. Sometimes, the large-scale event, radical cultural influx and ill-considered cultural investment provoked more negative than positive reactions in the community. This was because the events could threaten residents' living circumstances even though the cultural elements possessed positive potentiality with regard to developing the urban area" (S-3).

• What Happened in the Three Neighbourhoods After the CCEA?

Following the end of the CCEA, several events continued and were developed further, or events were newly created. Despite low correlation with the CCEA, a year-long event stimulated excitement and enthusiasm for existing events within Jungang-dong. After the CCEA moved to Daegu (a city in the North Gyeonsang Province), Cheongju Urban Regeneration Centre tried to create participative and co-operative cultural opportunities by placing resident involvement as a high priority. Such efforts acted as a dynamic force to increase self-confidence within the community and created a more positive acceptance of culture-led regeneration initiative than that which had come before.

In Naedeok-dong, a major cultural destination site during the CCEA, a range of new cultural programmes were held, and existing programmes were developed further than they had been before 2016 – around 30 main cultural events were managed, and the numbers of additional sub-programmes along with main events were significantly increased. Remarkably, as Cheongju was designated as 'the Special Zone for Culture' (SZC) from 2016 to 2020 (Cheongju ilbo, 2016), diversified cultural programmes took place in Naedeok-dong long after the end of the CCEA, to promote the SZC and distribute more cultural opportunities to residents. The CCEA was regarded as an opportunity for the cultural expansion of Naedeok-dong, and it also contributed to the launch of the 'Regional Development Project for Urban Revitalisation' in 2016. "Subsequent to the CCEA, there have been easily accessible programmes within the public square of CCIPF; it seemed that the distribution of equal cultural opportunities to the public was a principle priority in 2016" (N-3). "The formation of cultural programmes was made up of popular cultural events such as cinema screenings, performances, and exhibitions which were impressive enough to encourage ordinary people to become involved in cultural experiences" (N-1). In particular, Dongbu Storage (a storage facility owned by the Tobacco Factory, which was partially refurbished in 2015) provided space for performance rehearsals, a gallery, a local festival, a cinema, and a cultural forum during the CCEA. After the event, it became home to community-led events, arts festivals with local artist and culture classes.

Despite the low profile of the newly launched programmes in Suamgol, the popularity of them to the local community was still evident, with the location being home to a creative mural painting village and a film making location. The local council had plans to establish a drama theme park as a means by which to maintain Suamgol's popularity. In addition, the CCIPF announced 'the development for Suamgol healing road contents' that included Suamgol mobile contents, cartoons, media facades in the village, and the creation of a Suamgol character using coal briquette until the middle of 2017. However, there is still controversial debate on further cultural investments, with an argument raging as to whether creating a drama theme park is irrelevant to local development. Criticism focuses on the fact that the planning focuses solely on the influx of Chinese tourists fond of Korea drama and culture.

- The Legacy of the CCEA: Changing Cultural Perception Through Involving in or Experiencing Cultural Environment After the CCEA

"There have been few changes with regards to the cultural perceptions of residents. For some, culture and arts became an effective driver for vitalising life and supporting mental health" (J-1 and J-3). J-1 commented that he was a passive audience member during previous events. He also noted, however, how active cultural participation had allowed him to have vibrant feelings of the cultural atmosphere and produced mental refreshment. Furthermore, the power of culture included a potential to unify different generations: "it is inevitable that all generations have cultural diversity and differences. However, the cutting ceremony of the 1st Cheongju Pine-street Art Fair broke my perception that diverse generations from youngsters to the elderly could gather at one place with the same purpose. By attending this activity, I could feel that culture has an indefinite ability to harmonise all generation" (J-3).

Following the end of the 2015 CCEA, more high-quality community-based programmes emerged that were reasonably priced and offered a wide range of activities for children, adults and the elderly. This demonstrated an attempt to create a sustainable legacy Naedeok-dong's having been given the title 'cultural city'. The cultural events delivered since 2016 and the culture-driven economic regeneration projects pursued have helped develop this perception further. Between January and October 2016, more than 30 cultural opportunities were offered for a range of age groups. One respondent (N-2) said "after the CCEA, there were a number of family-centred programmes at the CCIPF. Such cultural offers encouraged more family bonding - belonging, connection and interaction between families - by playing all together, and it was a constructive opportunity to fasten solidarity between families". N 1 also felt that high-quality cultural programmes held within the open spaces in 2016 brought solidarity between neighbourhoods: "There were a number of events that offered a comfortable and relaxing environment to ordinary residents. Such a leisurely atmosphere was helpful in meeting new neighbours".

However, there were negative cultural perceptions of the events. N-3 insisted culture itself became more a discriminator after the large-scale event had gone: "I reckon that positive cultural perception could be achieved if people resided at around the main cultural venue or main cultural project area because I could not find any cultural benefits in 2016. For me, cultural projects sometimes tend to discriminate between participants and non-participants". Thus, the application of culture could be a positive influence in promoting constructive interactions with people, maximising local participation, and transferring the local image. Whereas, cultural resources tend to possess a dangerous factor that can be easily commercialised and privatised. Commercialisation by the culture and arts has advantages when it leads to improved infrastructure, increases associated business opportunities and enhances employment circumstances. However, the objections and outcry were prevalent amongst local residents because of a significant focusing on commercialisation and privatisation of the Tobacco Factory using cultural resources. In the same vein, sometimes cultural or artistic works accompany gentrification across Cheongju as well as South Korea. In this regard, cultural elements tend to be considered as an invisible weapon in the disadvantaged or poverty-stricken areas.

In the case of Suamgol, and despite the relatively low public awareness of the CCEA, Suamgol respondents still acknowledge the ability of culture to make the Suamgol community brighter than before: "Considerable deterioration on house and facilities has been ongoing without a break. The atmosphere of the community was unavoidably in the shade, but the steady cultural infusion helped Suamgol to escape from such negative images" (S-2). S-3 added that "in 2016, cultural programmes were not ceaseless in Suamgol. A few artists introduced new lifeblood into Suamgol, and such a brighter environment created by the cultural efforts generates a sense of pride, good neighbourliness, and a respecting of our community". However, S-3 voiced concern that culture is often considered as a trespasser of privacy: "The loss of privacy leads to mental distress, so some residents moved out due to stress of invasion of privacy". Further, Suamgol still suffered from a loss of authenticity by gentrification, with the phenomenon appearing to accelerate since the end of the CCEA: "As Cheongju is gaining cultural popularity, Suamgol is also highlighted along with Cheongju's reputation. In this sense, an influx of wealthier people and franchise businesses has gradually appeared around the community in 2016.

Further big cultural events might lead to Suamgol getting swept up in redevelopment initiatives or gentrification phenomenon. It is not a good feeling to give the village 50 years of my life. For me, sometimes, cultural elements have been regarded as a dread and anxiety" (S-2).

Table 6-2: Summary of perception changes regarding cultural projects

	General perceptions of cultural participation	Perception changes during and after the CCEA
Jungang-dong	• Driver for encouraging engagement • Playing an attractive role in designating an urban regeneration target area • Cultural participation is a waste of money and time • Hindrance for local business	• Capable of unifying people and promoting the community • Aid in reducing depression • Still a trigger for disrupting local business
Naedeok-dong	• Enriches residents' daily routines • Driver for developing local environment • Helper for changing deprived local image	• Helpful for family solidarity and cultural education • Catalyst for more active cultural businesses • Increased family or friend reunion opportunities • Enjoyable for all generations and communities • Provoked sense of discrimination between cultural participants and non-participants • Still invisible weapon that can bring privatisation and commercialisation
Suamgol	• Helpful in creating colourful environment and providing positive mind • Provide an unforgettable experience • Cultural elements can easily get popularity but can produce significant gentrification • Aid for reducing mental stress	• Still creator for bright local environment • Still aid for reducing mental stresses • Driver for attracting artistic popularity and visitors, but privacy invasion is inevitable • Enjoyable but not for the elderly

6.4 Summary

As one of the major culture-led urban regeneration strategies, the CCEA has been employed as a case study to prove the repercussions of culture-led urban regeneration strategies upon the declining areas of Cheongju, South Korea. This book has noted the debates which exist between local residents about the role of cultural events upon social regeneration using a qualitative approach. The opinions gathered from the field-research might become useful resources by which to recognise what social impacts emerged during and after the CCEA. Furthermore, the answers from residents who were immediately involved with the cultural programmes as well as the consequences of the regeneration projects may be helpful in developing future culture-led regeneration and social regeneration strategies. Finally, Table 6-2 shows a comparison of local residents' opinions about the CCEA in terms of community development and changes in the working environment can be found in Appendix 4.

Chapter 7

Lessons from the Culture-led Urban Regeneration Project: Through the CCEA

The intention of this book was to scrutinise the social regeneration dimensions of a cultural event and, through that, to reflect on the changing context of regeneration and culture-led regeneration in South Korea. There have been few findings pertaining to whether 'culture-led approaches created social regeneration opportunities in Cheongju and, if so, what opportunities and for whom?', 'what are the possible problem and tensions in using cultural events to support social regeneration in Cheongju?', 'how does the CCEA in Cheongju reinforce or challenge wider literature on the role of cultural events in social regeneration?'. In this Chapter, there are answers to these four questions as a conclusion of the book.

- Have culture-led approaches created social regeneration opportunities in Cheongju and, if so, what opportunities and for whom?

Through the CCEA, Cheongju city thrived as a cultural city, and its image evolved from a typical industrial city into one which secured a budget for cultural projects. However, in terms of creating social regeneration, the research found that the CCEA created limited social regeneration opportunities. There was some awareness and engagement with the CCEA amongst the respondents to this research, but it was mainly passive. This was particularly true of those in Naedeok-dong, (which hosted a range of major cultural venues). There tended to be more engagement from those sited within Jungang-dong and Suamgol.

It is true that during the CCEA, there were improvements to social cohesion through the voluntary works, community solidarity, cultural education for youth, skill development and acceptance of different cultures that took place. However, these social impacts were highly concentrated within Naedeok-dong. The other two areas experienced less tangible and less visible social impacts. The differences in the cultural perceptions of each of the three locations depended on the degree of cultural programmes in the areas, the previous experiences of cultural projects, the specific location characteristics, and the existing working or living circumstances of those who resided or worked therein. However, cultural perceptions are not easily changed through the hosting of a mega-event. In terms of community development by the CCEA, in general, survey participants considered that lasting and regular cultural events were associated with positive impacts and could help to create stable communities. Yet, the participants felt and saw that there had been little community development during the CCEA. During and after the CCEA, there is no doubt that multifarious cultural and artistic bodies were slipped into the three neighbourhoods, and that these assorted efforts contributed to a cultural vibrancy within the communities that had seldom been experienced before. In this regard, respondents felt that the CCEA retained its legacies across Cheongju's development. However, the positive degree of community development by the CCEA was (again) revealed mainly in Naedeok-dong. Respondents living in Naedeok-dong alluded more to affirmative community changes as the community benefitted from the plethora of CCEA programmes in 2015 and 2016. Due to the high density of CCEA programmes around the large cultural venues, the CCEA itself was viewed as being the latest catalyst in a line of explicitly culture-led regeneration initiatives

In light of the changes to living and working environments, it is concluded that the three research areas saw elements of cultural transition over the last few years. Following the end of the CCEA, artists and creators began to use derelict spaces and often transformed vacant spaces into artistic. Residents responded positively to such changes, saying the changes offered a more safe and comfortable set of living circumstances. However, the merchants interviewed in this research emphasised that the quantity and diversity of cultural projects were not imperative to local businesses or to reinforcing working environments. Further, many respondents experienced financial difficulties, and cultural events were not viewed as being significant in boosting their living circumstances. Clearly, any living or working environment can be developed if economic circumstances improve. The cultural benefits in the declining research areas were limited because the social regeneration aspects had been weak throughout the CCEA process. In addition, there had only been limited attempts to reach out, to connect, and to facilitate social regeneration during the event as a whole.

- What are the possible problems and tensions in using cultural events to support social regeneration in Cheongju?

The overriding finding from this research is that the social regeneration dimension is underdeveloped in the Cheongju CCEA. This can be traced to a range of factors. First, the CCEA was dominated by a narrow view of economic development and city promotion priorities. Undoubtedly, the 2015 CCEA was nominated as a result of political efforts and lobbying many stakeholders. However, as the urban development policy of Cheongju city has been considerably focused on issues of improving the economy and n physical development, citizens' cultural preferences and community needs were largely excluded from the CCEA process. This is not to say, of course, that economic development should not be a major element of urban improvement, and that the economic sphere is not essential in creating better lives. However, in the case of the CCEA, the significant weight placed on economic development and city promotion led to a lack of awareness and indifference amongst residents to the CCEA.

Many residents were unaware about the meanings of the CCEA, and could not answer questions as to why the events were being held in Cheongju, or how they could effectively participate in the programmes. . In this regard, ordinary residents could not realise the important social regeneration aspects within their communities that the CCEA offered. The top-down approach evident in the CCEA also impacted local businesses. During the CCEA, the number of contracts with big companies or businesses from other regions increased due to the strict restrictions that were placed on public organisations taking on the projects. This created chronic problems with local businesses facing difficulties participating in the large-sized cultural events; the structure of the event industry heavily relied on the bidding of public organisations, rather local companies. Although local merchants had a desire to be involved with the CCEA, the top-down approach provoked fund outflows and created a tardy development in the local working environment.

Finally, the CCEA was designed to create a cultural community between South Korea, China and Japan. It was believed that the nations could achieve positive effects through cultural exchange programmes in the aspects of politics, economy, social, culture, arts and science. However, the 2015 CCEA in Cheongju tended to use the exchange strategy as a political instrument, rather than its focused on coherent interactions between each nation's citizens. It could, therefore, be seen to have been an exercise in 'cultural democracy' rather than 'cultural exchange'. During the 2015 CCEA, the national event made efforts to inspire the city's status and enhance the city's image, rather than focusing primarily on citizens' engagement. Therefore, the cultural exchange programmes of the CCEA were confined to exhibitions, visiting performances of orchestras or contemporary dances and ballets, and traditional cultural experiences. As a result, the CCEA did not make art and culture accessible to a wider audience, and the national mega-event failed to encourage interactive relationships between city and citizens and fortified local culture and arts networks.

- How does the CCEA in Cheongju reinforce or challenge wider literature on the role of cultural events in social regeneration?

Major culture-led regeneration projects tend to focus on flagship city centre events with fairly limited outreach to deprived communities. In addition, such flagship events tend to act as anchors to commercial development and may leave areas with expensive white elephants for which new uses need to be found(Jones and Evans, 2008). In the light of the social regeneration created by cultural events, previous research has emphasised that cultural projects could bring new jobs to a city (direct, indirect and induced) (Evans, 2005; Jones and Evans, 2008 and Tallon, 2010). However, the CCEA failed to create job opportunities, as new jobs were often temporary and short-term. Moreover, CCEA-related jobs were already taken by and allocated to civil servants or someone directly involved in the events. Therefore, there was no attempt to achieve an equal distribution of job opportunities and no attempt to reduce ongoing unemployment.

Jones and Evans (2008) and Tallon (2010) also stress that cultural projects have the ability to generate extra spending in local economies (e.g. the leisure, arts and entertainment economy, and the development of the night-time economy). Such results were discovered in this research. However, the benefits were found to be concentrated around the main cultural venue areas (Naedeok-dong). Given the lack of distribution of cultural benefits to marginal communities during the CCEA, it was unsuccessful in enhancing the living and working circumstances of the research neighbourhoods. Finally, major events became a particular valuable in impacting city image and with regard to issues of local promotion (Richards and Wilson, 2004; Jones and Evans, 2008). In Cheongju, focusing on image change and a cultural influx provoked a distortion of locality, and the increase in tourists became a trigger for gentrification and the destruction of aspects of the existing community. Such an approach tends to ignore the community's actual needs and has limited economic or social benefits for residents.

- Lessons from wider existent literature on cultural events and their impacts on social regeneration

Although the 2015 CCEA in Cheongju sought to regenerate local areas through a cultural approach and via cultural exchange, it tended to view the initiative as a promotional tool for the city itself rather than as a priority for regeneration. Moreover, the CCEA was much more about regional development than urban regeneration. As the CCEA itself stated at an early stage, a key challenge to culture-led regeneration and its impacts on social regeneration aspects is the risk that it takes culture out of context and instrumentalises it for merely economic purposes - detached from geographical, temporal and local identity sensibilities (Garcia, 2013). Understanding the synergies as well as the conflicts that exist between economic, social and cultural sectors is necessary to maximise cultural events' potential and sustainability in the aspect of social regeneration by a cultural approach (reference here).

To boost social regeneration, arts and cultural events within regeneration projects should be "particularly keen on expressing the sustainable nature of their engagement with participants, seeing issues around sustainability as being primarily about the sustainability of the community with which they were engaged, rather than about the sustainability of themselves as an organisation" (Impacts 08, 2009, p. 27). As a nationally created event, the CCEA was created by the Cultural Ministers of South Korea, China and Japan. It reflected typical state-led and top-down cultural policies. As a result, there was little space to incorporate bottom-up strategies from residents or local cultural organisations. This made residents become passive participants to any policies, and they were unaware of the events held.

Furthermore, to promote the city internationally, almost all CCEA programmes were concentrated in the CCIPF, which was mainly managed by the local government. Residents already living around the main venue areas were the ones who benefitted culturally and socially, rather than residents from other, possibly more disadvantaged, areas (Impacts 08, 2010). To better develop a future CCEA project, there is a need to incorporate bottom-up cultural strategies, to ensure that cultural benefits are equally distributed between in central areas and marginal communities.

With regard to this particular point, the governance of ECOC Liverpool may be a particularly helpful example. In the process of ECOC, the arts and cultural sectors played an alternative leadership role alongside the regeneration agencies, such as Liverpool Vision and the Liverpool Arts Regeneration Consortium. In this way, they supplemented the Liverpool City Council, which had not properly integrated culture into its policies (O'Brien, 2011; Selwood, 2009). Particularly LARC was "an illustrative case of creative response to a perceived failure within the governance settlement for culture" in Liverpool (O'Brien,2011, p.55), and filled the gaps generated by the City Council's inertia regarding cultural policy-making In the same vein, Jepson and Clarke (2016) insist that in the beginning, public authorities are crucial, but that during the actual event, private and community stakeholders should take over network leadership. Misener and Mason (2006) also stress that local government bodies have to take a step back as their role changes from the regulator to facilitator during the overall process of an event. This process could strengthen communities and create solid networks between organisers and residents. A future CCEA should aim to build more joint partnerships to support the gap that exists between f central and local government with regards to cultural policies. Relying heavily on a state-led and top-down approach in the process of CCEA cannot reach out, connect to residents, or facilitate social regeneration.

- Implications for the management of future CCEA and improving social-led regeneration by a cultural approach

A key finding of this book for future practice is that social regeneration needs to be an explicit aim of cultural events, and must clearly identify who is to be involved, why and how, and include a programme of outreach and engagement. During the CCEA, the main challenge was to engage with individuals who were hard to reach and involve. In order to solve this challenge, gradual preparation, though resident-led processes should take place prior to hosting an event or undertaking a culture-led urban regeneration project. Respondents in this research did not want to experience merely one-off cultural events or symbolic cultural venues built as one aspect of culture-led regeneration projects. An accumulation of cultural experiences, constant cultural education in communities, and appropriate distribution of cultural opportunity over the years would gradually modify non-participants' attitudes and their perceptions of such processes.

It is believed that organisers and stakeholders often neglected the needs of community and residents in the shadow of generating their own benefits and achievements when creating the CCEA. Theoretical and practical cultural elements within urban development have multiplier impacts within an economy and impact social spheres such as jobs, income/expenditure, inward investment, distributive effects, community cohesion, increasing social capital, and reducing the crime rate and the fear of crime (Evans, 2005). However, many respondents involved in the research that underpins this book stressed the fact that they could not recognise and had not noticed direct economic and social benefits emanating from the CCEA or d previous culture-led regeneration projects. They tended instead to consider economic and social impacts as being simply theory. Such answers indicate that future CCEA management and culture-led regeneration initiatives should find common ground to bridge cultural programmes, local economy (as being not only for the city economy) and social improvements.

Finally, in general, respondents acknowledged the importance of experts who come from the government and practical fields to intervene in future community strategies. However, local residents often pointed out that while the knowledge and skills of experts are useful, they do not indicate how local residents use cultural strategies or reflect local business for community sustainability. Organisers and policymakers should establish effective ways for local residents to benefit from the events and regenerative projects. For residents, the theory and abstract of cultural impact on social regeneration are not important; it is the visible outcomes and practical engagement that matter to them.

- Importance of joined-up thinking between different agencies

In the theory of culture-led urban regeneration, well-organised and well-structured partnerships are emphasised as being decisive factors leading to success and further sustainability (Garcia, 2004; Sharp, Pollock and Paddison, 2005; Timur and Getz. 2008). Authors stress that a cultural approach project should establish a partnership with public, private and residents to sustain long-term benefits in communities. By reviewing the CCEA, it can be noted that the committee structure between public, private and the community remained controversial in terms of the establishment of effective partnerships. When the committee was organised to support the event, it was managed by representatives from local authorities, universities, the health and education sectors, and a broadcast company along with several other state and non-state actors. There was no space for residents or community level stakeholders (e.g. charitable sectors or ordinary people) in the entire CCEA 2015 process.

Jones and Evans (2008) stress that "the rhetoric of joined-up thinking between different agencies is laudable and ensuring that socially deprived areas are targeted for improvements in education, health and public safety entirely sensible" (p. 20). With regard to this specific point, the CCEA tended to be mainly operated by central government departments containing central-driven priorities which could not tackle intractable social problems in inner cities. The intervention of non-state agents, voluntary community participation and the active involvement of ordinary people would be an effective way to secure social regeneration beyond the CCEA development. In particular, co-operation with the intermediate organisation 'Urban Regeneration Supporting Centre' could be a key driver to unite the range of diverse ideas, and enable the sharing of common features as well as the coordination of culture-led regeneration programmes and cultural events at the mass level in South Korea. During the 2015 CCEA, there was no direct linkage with the Cheongju urban regeneration supporting the centre. Given that this centre had been established to regenerate declining areas, a close relationship could have resulted in great synergy with regards to developing the CCEA's management as well as with regards to social regeneration aspects.

Summary

This book sought to provide an understanding of the social regeneration impacts of a cultural event, the CCEA of Cheongju, and to explore the influence that had upon deprived communities. It also provides a snapshot of South Korea's current urban regeneration policies, including those pertaining to culture-led regeneration and the changing nature of approaches to urban policy from urban redevelopment to urban regeneration. To address the existent research gap within the literature on culture-led urban regeneration in South Korea, empirical evidence generated from the answers and opinions of twenty-one experts was explored to show how current culture-led regeneration initiatives have been formulated. Those practical and realistic answers provide for a much sturdier comprehension of the meaning of culture-led regeneration, as well as enabling a greater understanding of the current. With regards to the relationship between social regeneration factors and cultural events, this study addressed an existent gap in South Korean and international literature. By utilising the qualitative methods, the work allows for a deeper understanding of social factors that are inherent within complex societies. During the field-research, it emerged that the CCEA and the term 'culture-led urban regeneration' are both unfamiliar topics in general with respondents. The qualitative approach offered people an opportunity to create their own responses, to voice their own views and vividly drew detailed feelings and attitudes towards cultural engagement and social regeneration aspects. When the quantitative approach is used for social research by cultural events, these realistic and authentic opinions can easily be excluded. However, in this social regeneration research, local residents were given top priority to widen an understanding as to how people realistically consider a cultural approach to regenerating areas and the impacts that such an approach has on communities and individual environments.

Appendix 1
Resident Participation

To obtain realistic answers from residents of the targeted areas, 121 questionnaires were distributed with an important criterion being the need to focus on those who have lived within the targeted area for at least 20 years. This criterion was important because it enabled the author to obtain an insight into how residents/participants had observed culture-led regeneration projects or events within their communities, and enabled the author to access their knowledge about the community's needs and local cultural value - 74 answers were returned. The demographic statistics of the participants are outlined below.

Categories		Numbers	%	Categories		Numbers	%
Gender	Male	30	40.5	Employ-ment Status	Employee	27	36.4
	Female	44	59.5		Civil servant	5	6.7
					Homemaker	11	14.8
Age groups	30s	5	6.7		Own business	14	18.9
	40s	14	18.9		Others	17	22.9
	50s	20	27				
	60s	23	31	Period of Residence	20-30 years	23	31
	Over 70s	12	16.2		30-40	25	33.8
					40-50	28	37.8
Marriage Status	Married	64	86.4		Over 50	8	10.8
	Single	10	13.5				

Amongst questionnaire participants, 26 respondents accepted invitations to take part in short interviews after their questionnaires had been completed. The interviews were semi-structured with open-ended and topic-centred questions. The questions reflected an open-ended format, so respondents could answer flexibly in their own terms, without being forced to produce a certain kind of answer. Interviewees' specific information has been formulated and can be used to better understand how the respondents regarded culture-led urban regeneration.

	Gender *Male: M Female: F	Age Groups	Cultural participant between 2011-2014	CCEA participant	Employment Status	Period of Residence (years)
J-1	M	50s	X	X	Own Business	30-40
J-2	F	60s	O	O	Homemaker	30-40
J-3	F	50s	X	O	Employee	20-30
J-4	M	60s	O	X	Own Business	30-40
J-5	M	50s	O	O	Employee	20-30
J-6	F	50s	X	X	Resident*	40-50
J-7	M	60s	X	O	Resident	30-40
J-8	F	40s	O	O	Homemaker	20-30
J-9	F	50s	O	X	Own Business	20-30
J-10	M	60s	X	X	Employee	30-40
N-1	M	50s	X	X	Own Business	30-40
N-2	F	50s	O	O	Employee	20-30
N-3	M	60s	O	O	Employee	20-30
N-4	F	50s	X	O	Homemaker	30-40
N-5	F	60s	X	X	Resident	30-40
N-6	M	60s	O	O	Own Business	40-50
N-7	F	50s	O	X	Resident	30-40
N-8	F	40s	O	O	Homemaker	20-30
S-1	F	60s	O	X	Homemaker	30-40
S-2	F	70s	O	O	Resident	30-40
S-3	M	80s	X	O	Resident	Over 50
S-4	M	70s	O	X	Employee	30-40
S-5	F	80s	X	X	Resident	20-30
S-6	M	70s	O	X	Own Business	40-50
S-7	F	70s	O	X	Resident	40-50
S-8	F	80s	X	X	Resident	Over 50

* 'J' refers to Jungang-dong, 'N' refers to Naedeok-dong, and 'S' refers to Suamgol

Appendix 2
SWOT Analysis for Understanding Cheongju

	STRENGTH	WEAKNESS
Internal origin **External origin**	- Located in the heart of the National space and - Metropolitan transportation - The centre of the high-tech Industry - Has a beautiful national environment, and various historical and cultural assets - Possesses agricultural infrastructure and plenty of demand in local xxx - Build the high-tech industry	- Imbalance between city centre and suburb areas - Impossible the coast transit due to geographical position - Generates NIMBYism against landfill sites, incineration plants and other disposal facilities - Increase thoughtless development in suburb areas - Absence of long-term strategies for Cheongju - Industrial Complex
OPPORTUNITY	**Strength-Opportunity STRATEGY**	**Weakness-Opportunity STRATEGY**
- Promote the government-supported national development project - Create the environment friendly area - Activates urban regeneration initiatives as a national priority strategy	- Formulate counterstrategy for transferring government offices - Systematically develop tourist attractions and cultural spaces - Foster the city as a gateway of capitals - Promote new growth industry in connection with core industries	- Develop urban-rural integration projects - Harmonise regions through discovering local industries - Appropriately allocate noxious facilities - Promote urban regeneration scheme using the national core policies - Build a supply complex
THREAT	**Strength-Threat STRATEGY**	**Weakness-Threat STRATEGY**
- Grow the adjacent city's competitiveness and strength - Depressed the construction and development business due to a property recession - Increasing low birth rate and ageing population	- Seek mutual cooperation with the adjacent cities (ex: Industry-Academia partnership, research and development (R&D) institution and High-tech industrial complex) - Foster the culture and tourism industries - Improve the urban areas through gradual small-scale project - Revitalise the agroecosystem	- Advance industrial structure within abandoned industrial area - Establish the counterplan to reduce thoughtless development in suburban areas - Enhance the educational and learning environments - Reinforce the welfare system keeping pace with the era of low birth rate and ageing population

Source: 2030 Cheonjgu Urban Master Plan (2014) (Translated by the author)

Appendix 3

The CCEA Programmes in Cheongju

	Programmes	Date	Location	Organiser
Special Event	• Culture Forum of three nations - Visit the cultural facilities - Find and investigate culture-related development issues and marketing strategies	June	Cheongju cultural industry promotion foundation	Ministry of Culture, Sports and Tourism
	• Tourism conference of Korea and Japan - The celebration of 50th normalisation of diplomatic relation between Korea and Japan - Consult about tourism promotion and improvement - Tour at the international craft Biennale, organic Expo and university of Cheongnam	September	Cheongju	Cheongju City Council
	• Culture partnership business - Invite 50 culture and art experts who work in the developing countries (e.g. the Azerbaijani Republic, Vietnam, Mongolia, etc.) - Form a network with artists - Visit Korea's cultural attraction - Attend a Korean language class - Take place joint performance	July ~ August	Cheongju	Chungbuk Artist Federation
Partner-ship Events	• 13th Cheongju arts festival - Exhibition - Academic conference - Performance - Jikji marathon	April	Cheongju Art Centre	Chungbuk Artist Federation
	• Spring Culture Festival Cultural experience and concerts	April	National Cheongju Museum	Cheongju Artist Federation
	• Youth Festival Dance, playing and singing competition	April	Cheongju	Cheongju Artist Federation
	• Cheongju Arts Festival Performance, exhibition, arts competition	April	Musimcheon	Cheongju Artist Federation

• Academic event - Forum for municipal region's airport within East Asia - Forum for East Asia's urban regeneration	April ~ May	Cheongju and Ningbo, China	Chungbuk development research centre
• Exhibition event Traditional culture and artworks exhibition of three nations	May		Cheongju cultural industry promotion foundation
• East Asian Network – East Asia culture market	Mat	Cheongju	Ministry of Culture, Sports and Tourism
• The World Day for Cultural Diversity for Dialogue and Development concert, craft, cinema, drawing, seminars for returning to farms, theatre, food festival, Buggy parade, citizen society competition, etc.	May	Cheongju cultural industry promotion foundation	Cheongju cultural industry promotion foundation
• Flea market	May (every Saturday)	Jungang-dong Market street	
• King Sejong and Chojeong water festival - symposium about letter and civilisation - Royal ceremonial walk	May	Chojeong Water park	Cheongju cultural foundation
• The 22nd Cheongju Art Festival - Joint traditional performance with Korea, Japan, China, Vietnam and Mongol - Concert of each nation - Watching movie - Folk painting exhibition	August	Cheongju Art Centre	Chungbuk Artist Federation, and Cheongju City Council
• Cheongju Fortress Festival - Historical performance for Citizen's victory - Food festival - Singing festival for youth - A great religious ceremony for commemorate - Jikji music concert	September	Around Seongan-street	Cheongju City Council and Cheongju Cultural Federation
• 2015 Cheongju International Craft Biennale - International exhibition - Craft conference - Craft fair - Artworks of three nations' youth	September ~ October	Tobacco Factory in Naedeok-dong	Biennale committee

- Various concert and performance during the Biennale			
• Guryoung Festival	September	University of Sewon	Cheongju
• Cheongwon life festival - Agricultural product market - Agricultural experience event - Various concerts - More than 60 practical programmes related to agriculture	October	Ochang Miraeji Park	Life festival Committee
• Chungbuk Arts Festival	October	Cheongju	Chungbuk Artist Federation
• The Festival for Chinese Student	October	The Cheongju Arts Hall	Chungcheong-bukdo
• East Asia music festival 'From East Wind' (Korea, Japan, Vietnam and Mongol)	November	Cheongju Art hall	
• Chopstick festival - Chopstick performance - Academic forum about chopsticks of three nations - East Asia chopstick exhibition - Chopstick related game	November	Cheongju cultural industry promotion foundation	Cheongju City council, Cheongju cultural industry promotion foundation, and CCEA
• Exhibition events - The four-ceremonial occasion festival (coming of age, wedding, funeral and ancestral rites) - Modern art exhibition of three nations	November ~ December	Cheongju cultural industry promotion foundation, Daecheong-ho gallery	Cheongju cultural industry promotion foundation, and Art Chungbuk
• Performance events - Art company's performance of three nations - Joint performance - Citizen-led performance - Civic group and Cheongju's art society performance	December	Cheongju Arts Centre	

[source: author]

Appendix 4

Summary of Residents' Opinions about the CCEA in terms of Community Development and Changes to Living and Working Environments

JUNGANG-DONG			
	BEFORE the CCEA	DURING the CCEA	AFTER the CCEA
POSITIVE	• Car-free zone projects and hosting cultural events in the zone vibrantly transformed the market street • Floating population increased • Community-based programmes helped the community environment to flourish • A solid cultural project (e.g. flea market and busking) enhanced resident participation • The rate of un-occupied buildings has decreased	• A lot of media attention with hosting mega-event in Cheongju is a great opportunity to promote Jungang-dong's potential and cultural capability	• After the CCEA, more extended and developed programmes were introduced than the period of CCEA, and a more vibrant and youthful environment has been formed compared to that which existed before 2015 • Urban regeneration agency and cultural organisations have made more efforts than before with regard to community development • There are plenty of cultural works in unused spaces
NEGATIVE	• Merely a cultural approach could not tackle socio-economic problems of the community (e.g. unemployment and repair of housing) • No striking differences are made by culture and arts • Car-free zone for cultural event stimulated to decrease of consumer • No advantages to ordinary people	• Inappropriate delivery of the CCEA made no difference to community development • CCEA stimulates thinking about 'whose culture' in the process of mega-event • Although it is a large-size event, the benefits flow in the political elites and organisers rather than community	• Quantity and variety of cultural project are not important to local business and residents • Economic improvement should be formed with cultural resources for community development and improving living and working environment

		• Difficult to say that mega-event can improve housing condition, reduce crime rate and healthiness	
• NAEDEOK-DONG			
POSITIVE	• Plentiful cultural offers attract more cultural investment for community development (e.g. CCEA and economic-led urban regeneration) • Unused factory is transfigured by the cultural influx, and the surrounding environment has become brighter	• There are volunteering opportunities and programmes for promoting community cohesion during the CCEA • This is the way that residents can take full ownership of cultural programmes • Lots of community-based programmes provide collective memory opportunities between residents • It helps to change the image of Naedeok-dong • The income benefits of big festivals rippled throughout the local economy • Create revenue by the growth of nightlife • A number of parade and street performance give a safer and more comfortable feeling • Cultural environment deters for crime and violence during the CCEA	• Still, various events are ongoing along with the vibrant cultural atmosphere • CCEA became a momentum in drawing more cultural investment to Naedeok-dong's streets • After the CCEA, local artists started to settle down at unoccupied places in Naedeok-dong, and provided productive cultural opportunities for residents
NEGATIVE	• Cultural leverage does not reach community level • Culture and arts are a catalyst for privatisation and the commercialisation of the local area • Unreasonable cultural injections spoil local features and hamper community development	• It focuses heavily on city promotion, encourages cultural consumption, and generates benefits to specific people or organisations. • Mega-event stimulates discriminatory feelings between participants and non-participants	• Extended cultural investment is still threatening the existence of local businesses

	• Cultural action has the intention to achieve the profit for private companies and interrupt the growth of the local working environment		
• **SUAMGOL**			
POSITIVE	• Cultural projects changed the image of the community from a shantytown to a culturally vibrant community • Cultural popularity also helped to escape the image of deprivation • Cultural transformation was a key way to sustain the community (e.g. opening the local shop by local residents) • Culture-led project increases visitors' spending • Energetic environment gives more enjoyment to elderly	• People cannot recognise community development during the CCEA due to low awareness about the CCEA	• More artists are attracted into the vacant places and have created their work there since 2016 • Such trial would be helpful in reducing crime and drug rates of young people
NEGATIVE	• Gentrification has been radically raised • Artistic works sometimes threaten the existing local culture • Along with cultural development, new investment (e.g. building a café, franchised-restaurant) is increased, but it destructs community living and working environment • Residents' privacy is at risk by tourists	• There is a tendency that thoughtless cultural works are invested along with mega-event (e.g. statues of actors) • Although the mega-event is hosted in Cheongju, residents are not at ease from crime threats and unsafe living circumstances	• Gentrification is still the biggest concern in this community after the CCEA

[Author]

Bibliography

Ahn, S. (2016). Ever expanding Cheongju, a stride towards global life culture city [online]. Translated from Korean. *Chungbuk Newspaper.* Updated 13 June 2016, 15:01. [Viewed 25 October 2017]. Available from: http://www.inews365.com/news/article.html?no=451182

An, S. (2015). The acceleration of deprivation in Cheongju [online]. Translated from Korean. *Chungbuk Newspaper.* Updated 21 January 2015. 19:42:20. [Viewed: 14 March 2017]. Available from: http://www.inews365.com/news/article.html?no=380739

Asian Development Bank. (2012). *The Saemaul Undong movement in the Republic of Korea: sharing Knowledge on Community-Driven Development.*

Bianchini, F. and Parkinson, M. (1993). *Cultural policy and urban regeneration: The west european experience.* Manchester University Press.

Byun, W. (2015). 'Introduce the community's delicious restaurant' as the one of the Culture City of East Asia event programme [online]. Translated by Korean. *Yeonhap Newspaper.* Updated 24 September 2015, 08:54. [Viewed 17 October 2016]. Available from: http://www.yonhapnews.co.kr/bulletin/2015/09/24/0200000000AKR20150924027900064.HTML?in put=1195m

Carter, A. (2000). Strategy and partnership in urban regeneration. In P. Roberts, and H. Sykes. ed. *Urban Regeneration A Hand Book.* SAGE.

CCEA website. (2015a). Build the CCEA global networks [online]. Translated from Korean. *CCEA website.* Updated 2 November 2015. [Viewed 4 May 2016]. Available from: http://www.culturecj.com/single-post/2015/11/02/%EB%8F%99%EC%95%84%EC%8B%9C%EC%95%84%EB%AC%B8%ED%99%94%EB%8F%84%EC%8B%9C-%EA%B8%80%EB%A1%9C%EB%B2%8C%EB%84%A4%ED%8A%B8%EC%9B%8C%ED%81%AC%EB%A7%9D-%EA%B5%AC%EC%B6%95

City of Yokohama News Release. (2014). *Culture City of East Asia 2014, YOKOHAMA – Japan-China-Korea Youth Cultural Exchange Project* [online]. [Viewed 5 October 2016]. Available from: http://www.city.yokohama.lg.jp/ex/mayor/interview/pressroom/newsrelease/h26/20140829newsrelease-e.pdf

Cheongju ilbo. (2016). Successful first step forward as a cultural city of Cheongju [online]. Translated from Korean. *Cheongju ilbo.* Updated 26 December. [Viewed 17 June 2017]. Available at: http://www.cj-ilbo.com/news/articleView.html?idxno=930640

Choi, J. (2016). Eco-friendly agricultural products from local farmers all in one place, also plenty of 'hands on' experiences [online]. Translated from Korean. *Jungang Newspaper.* Updated 21 September 2016, 00:01. [Viewed 13 February 2017]. Available from: http://news.joins.com/article/20613057

Chungbuk in News. (2014). O-Young Lee is co-opted as av-chairman for the Cultural City of East Asia [online]. Translated from Korean. *Chungbuk in news.* Updated: 20 December 2014, 17:24. [Viewed: 22 November 2016]. Available from: http://www.cbinews.co.kr/news/articleView.html?idxno=99950

Comedia. (2003). *Releasing the cultural potential of our core cities: culture and the core cities* [online]. Available from: http://www.corecities.com/coreDEV/comedia/com_cult.html

Couch, C. (1990). *Urban renewal: theory and practice.* Macmillan.

Craggs, R. (2008). *Tourism and urban regeneration: An analysis of visitor perception, behaviour and experience at the Quays in Salford.* Management and Management Sciences Research Institute.

Derry City Council. (n.d.). *Peace Bridge.* Available from: http://www.derrycity.gov.uk/peacebridge/Peace-Bridge

Derry City Council. (2009). *Derry-Londonderry Candidate City UK City of Culture 2013: Our bid, Derry-Londonderry.*

Ennis, N. and Douglass, G. (2011). *Culture and regeneration – What evidence is there of a link and how and can it be measured?* Glaeconomics. Greater London Authority.

Evans, G. and Shaw, P. (2004). *The contribution of culture to regeneration in the UK: A review of evidence.* A report to the Department for Culture Media and Sport. London Metropolitan University.

Evans, G. (2005). Measure for measure: Evaluating the evidence of culture's contribution to regeneration, *Urban Studies,* 42 (5/6): pp. 959-983.

Fisher, R. (2014). *South Korea country report. Preparatory action culture in EU external relations.* European Union [online]. Available from: http://ec.europa.eu/assets/eac/culture/policy/international-cooperation/documents/country-reports/south-korea_en.pdf

Foreign Press Centre Japan. (2013). *City of Yokohama: Officially designated as a "Cultural City of East Asia 2014".* Available from: http://fpcj.jp/en/useful-en/wjn-en/p=16427/

Garcia, B. (n.d.). *Looking in on the City. Liverpool as Capital of Culture: Impacts and effects* [online]. Available from: https://www.liverpool.ac.uk/media/livacuk/impacts08/pdf/pdf/BG(2008-09)BA-LookingInOnCity.pdf

Garcia, B. (2004). Cultural policy and urban regeneration in western European cities: Lessons from experience, prospects for the future. *Local Economy.* Vol. 19, No. 4, pp. 312-326.

Garcia, B. (2013). *Evaluating the impact of major cultural events.* Scottish cultural evidence network seminar. Edinburgh, 26 April 2013.

Garcia, B., Melville, R. and Cox, T. (2010). *Creating an impact: Liverpool's experience as European Capital of Culture.* University of Liverpool.

Gill, J. (2011). Legislative review for urban regeneration special Act. *Journal of Land method of construction research.* Vol. 53, pp. 1-24.

Ginsburg, N. (1999). Putting the social into urban regeneration policy. *Local economy.* Vol.14, pp. 55-71.

Greene, S. J. (2003). Staged cities: Mega-events, slum clearance, and global capital. *Yale Human Rights and Development Journal.* Vol. 6: Issue. 1, Article 6.

Guideline for EXPO 2012 Yeosu Korea. (n.d.). *Things to watch and enjoy at Yeosu Expo from A to Z.* Translated from Korean. Available from: http://eng.expo2012.kr/exponas/psfile/images_en/main/guideLine.pdf

Gwangju Activity Report. (2015). *The Gwangju encyclopaedia about the Culture City of East Asia.* [online]. Translated from Korean. Available from: http://file.tcs-asia.org/file_manager/files/tcs/6.%20Human%20and%20Cultural%20Exchange/4.%20Korean/1.%20%EB%AC%B8%ED%99%94/Gwangju%20Activity%20Report.pdf

Haenam Newspaper. (2006). Raise the best village in Jinan-gun [online]. Translated from Korean. *Haenam Newspaper*. Updated 23 June 2006. 00:00:00. [Viewed 24 May 2016]. Available from: http://www.hnews.co.kr/news/articleView.htm?idxno=11714

Hankyoreh. (2012). The half success of Yeosu Expo, focus on ex post facto management [online]. Translated from Korean. *Hankyoreh*. Updated 12 August 2012, 19:06. [Viewed 6 November 2017]. Available from: http://www.hani.co.kr/arti/opinion/editorial/546757.html

Hong, K. (2013). *South Korea / 5.2. legislation on culture* [online]. World CP website. Updated: 29 November 2013. [Viewed 3 November 2017]. Available from: http://www.worldcp.org/southkorea.php?aid=52

Hong, K. (2013a). *South Korea / 1. Historical perspective: cultural policies and instruments* [online]. World CP website. Updated: 29 November 2013. [Viewed 3 November 2017]. Available from: http://www.worldcp.org/southkorea.php

Human and Community. (2012). *The 2012 Report of Seongmisan village research.*

Impacts 08. (2010). Neighbourhood Impacts.

Isak (2015). Embarking on urban regeneration project backed by the conglomerate investment...opposition of civic group concerning the destroy of local economy [online]. Translated from Korean. *Kyeonghang newspaper.* Updated 9 March 2015. 16:40:44. [Viewed 4 July 2016]. Available from: http://news.khan.co.kr/kh_news/khan_art_view.html?artid=201503091640441&code=620111

Jepson, A. and Clarke, A. (2016). *Managing and Developing Communities, Festivals and Events*. PALGRAVE MACMILLAN.

Jones, P. and Evans, J. (2008). *Urban regeneration in the UK*. SAGE publications

Joo, Y. Bae, Y. and Kassens-Noor, E. (2017*). Mega-events and mega-ambitions: South Korea's rise and the strategic use of the big four events*. Palgrave Macmillan.

Jung, A. (2017). Ministry of Land, Infrastructure and Transport's urban regeneration project leads to increase tourism in Gunsan [online]. Translated from Korean. *Asiatoday*. Updated 27 February 2017. 14:31. [Viewed 20 March 2017]. Available from: http://www.asiatoday.co.kr/view.php?key=20170227010017938

Kang, M. (2014). *Introducing the Special Act on urban regeneration: Urban regeneration as the change of urban redevelopment paradigm*. Ministry of Government Legislation.

Kim, B. (2010). Prior tasks and future of urban regeneration [online]. Translated from Korean. The *Housingherald*. Updated 11 June 2010. 20:11. [Viewed 3 March 2016]. Available from: http://www.housingherald.co.kr/news/articleView.html?idxno=2171

Kim, J. (2015a). 'Hand craft' captivates 310,000 audiences and draws to a merry finale [online]. Translated from Korean. *Dongyang Newspaper*. Updated 25 October 2015, 20:38. [Viewed 3 March 2017]. Available from: http://m.dynews.co.kr/news/articleView.html?idxno=283221

Kim, K. (2015). Bring the relationship by destroying the house wall [online]. Translated from Korean. *Ohmy News*. Updated 3 September 2015, 12:14. [Viewed 6 November 2017]. Available from: http://www.ohmynews.com/NWS_Web/View/at_pg.aspx?CNTN_CD=A0001087617

Kim, S. (2012). 8million visitor milestone reached, but short of blockbuster success. Why? [online]. Translated from Korean. *News1*. Updated 9 August 2012. 05:13. [Viewed 21 March 2017]. Available from: http://news1.kr/articles/?771412

Kim, S. (2015b). City of Cheongju, initiatives for local talent-sharing events throughout the Culture City of East Asia [online]. Translated from Korean. *Chungbuk Newspaper*. Updated 5 May 2015, 17:09. [Viewed 23 October 2016]. Available from: http://www.inews365.com/news/article.html?no=395407

Kim, T. (2017). Jeonju Hanok village visitor numbers hit the record levels, over ten million [online]. Translated from Korean. *Asia economy*. Updated: 13 February 2013, 18:15. [Viewed 5 November 2017]. Available from: http://www.asiae.co.kr/news/view.htm?idxno=2017021318132111363

Kim, Y. (1976). *Cultural policy in the Republic of Korea*. UNESCO.

Kivlehan, N. (2013). Derry looks to capitalise on culture [online]. *Data, News & Analysis*. Updated: 17 May 2013. [Viewed 24 July 2016]. Available from: http://www.egi.co.uk/news/article.aspx?id=766916

Korea Research Institute for Human Settlements. (2012*). Liveable City Making: results and challenge of pioneering areas*. Translated from Korean.

Kyung, S. and Kim, K. J. (2011). 'State-facilitated Gentrification' in Seoul, South Korea: for Whom, by Whom and with What Result?. *Proceeding of the international RC21 conference 2011*, Amsterdam. Retrieved from http://www.rc21.org/conferences/amsterdam2011/edocs/Session%202/2-1-Kyung.pdf

Landry, C. and Greene, L. and Matarasso, F. and Bianchini, F. (1996). *The Art of Regeneration: Urban Renewal through Cultural Activity*. COMEDIA.

Lee, E. and Kim, K. (2016). Livable city making in Samdeok-dong Daegu [online]. Translated from Korean. *Urbanplanning*. Updated 22 April 2016. 13:56. [Viewed 21 March 2017]. Available from: http://modesty6878.tistory.com/1

Lee, I. (2016). Publishing the 2015 official social survey of Cheongju [online]. Translated from Korean. *Gukjenews*. Updated 15 January 2016. 07:27:12. [Viewed 20 May 2016]. Available from: http://www.gukjenews.com/news/articleView.html?idxno=408763

Lee, J. (2016a). From depression to hopeful circumstance… Jungang-dong is revived as a mecca of culture and arts [online]. *ChosunBiz*. Updated 24 February 2016. 06:45. [Viewed 10 November 2017]. Available from: http://biz.chosun.com/site/data/html_dir/2016/02/23/2016022302853.html

Lee, K. (2007). Questioning a neoliberal urban regeneration policy: the rhetoric of "Cities of Culture" and the City of Gwangju, Korea. *The International Journal of Cultural Policy 12 (4)*. University of Wollongong.

Lee, S. (2013). Jungang-dong in Cheongju became the mecca of urban regeneration [online]. Translated from Korea. *Newsis*. Updated 28 July 2013. [Viewed 12 July 2016]. Available from: http://news.joins.com/article/12188633

Legislation. (2011). *The urban and residential environment improvement act enforcement ordinance* [online]. Translated from Korean. Available from: http://www.law.go.kr/lsInfoP.do?lsiSeq=111797&efYd=undefined#0000

Lim, K. (2015). *Liveable community project and socio-economic* [online]. Translated from Korean. *JES*. http://s-space.snu.ac.kr/bitstream/10371/95544/1/04%20%EC%9E%84%EA%B2%BD%EC%88%98.pdf

Lim, S. (2013). Urban and residential environment improvement act is needed urgent amendment [online]. Translated from Korean. *Chungcheong Times.* Updated 10 September 2013. [Viewed 7 March 2016]. Available from: http://www.cctimes.kr/news/articleView.html?idxno=347573

Matarasso, F. (1997). *Use or ornament? The social impact of participation in the arts.* COMEDIA.

Matarasso, F and Landry, C. (1999). *Balancing Act: 21 strategic dilemmas in cultural policy.* Cultural policies research and development unit. Policy Note No. 4. Council of Europe.

McCarthy, J. (2007). *Partnership, collaborative planning and urban regeneration.* Ashgate.

Ministry of Culture and Information. (1979). *Culture and communication for 30 years.* (1948 – 1978).

Ministry of Land, Infrastructure and Transport. (2015). The development research for the 2014 City Vitality Promotion project.

Ministry of Landscape, Infrastructure and Transport Website. (n.d.). *Activation and support for urban regeneration* [online]. Translated from Korean. Available from: http://www.molit.go.kr/USR/WPGE0201/m_35396/DTL.jsp

Misener, L., and Mason, D.S. (2006). Creating community networks: Can sporting events offer meaningful sources of social capital? *Managing Leisure,* 11, pp. 39–56.

Mooney, G. (2004). Cultural policy as urban transformation? Critical reflections on Glasgow, European City of Culture 1990. *Local Economy.* 19, pp. 327-340.

Myerscough, J. (1991). *Monitoring Glasgow 1990.* Report for Glasgow City Council, Strathclyde Regional Council and Scottish Enterprise.

Nam, I. (2015). Cheongju depicts the dream of City of Culture: the centre of the world [online]. Translated from Korean. *Seoul Newspaper.* Updated 13 April 2015, 03:07. [Viewed 2 February 2017]. Available from: http://news.naver.com/main/read.nhn?mode=LSD&mid=sec&oid=081&aid=0002545946&sid1=001

Newsis. (2014). Chungbuk, increasing ageing rate in Cheongju... The emergency for tackling ageing society [online]. Translated from Korean. *Newsis.* Updated 28 December 2016. 13:27:04. [Viewed 20 March 2017]. Available from: http://mobile.newsis.com/view.html?ar_id=NISX20141001_0013205394

Northall, P. (n.d.). *Culture Led Regeneration & Local Art Communities.* Centre for Local Economic Strategies.

O'Brien, D. (2011). Who is in charge? Liverpool, European Capital of Culture 2008 and the governance of cultural planning. *The Town Planning Review.* Vol. 82, No. 1.

Pre-2014 Asia Culture Forum (2014). *Mutual growth of Asia and East Asia City of Culture.* Translated from Korean. Chonnam National University, Yongbong Hall.

Roberts, P. (2000). The evolution, definition and purpose of urban regeneration. In: P. Roberts and H. Skyes, ed. *Urban Regeneration A Handbook.* SAGE, pp. 9-36.

Richards, G. and Wilson, J. (2004). The impact of cultural events on city image: Rotterdam, Cultural Capital of Europe 2001. *Urban Studies,* Vol. 41, No. 10, pp. 1931-1951. Carfax Publishing.

Scott, L. (1995). When push comes to shove: Forced evictions and human rights. *Habitat International Coalition*, pp. 29 – 30.

Seo, S. and Yoon, J. (2015). *The suggestions of improvement schemes for urban regeneration Act.* Translated from Korean. AURIC.

Seo, S. Park, S. and Lim, K. (2014). *Operation strategies for the national urban regeneration assistant agency.* Architecture & Urban Research Institute. Available from: http://dlps.nanet.go.kr/DlibViewer.do?cn=MONO1201545435&sysid=nhn

Sharp, J., Pollock, V. and Paddison, R. (2005). Just art for a just city: Public art and social inclusion in urban regeneration. *Urban Studies.* 42(5/6), pp.1001-1023.

Shaw, K. (2016). Urban regeneration & sustainability. In: C.A. Brebbia, and A. Galiano-Garrigos. ed. *Urban Regeneration and Sustainability.* WIT Press.

Shin, H. and Stevens, Q. (2013). How culture and economy meet in South Korea: the politics of cultural economy in culture-led urban regeneration. *International Journal of Urban and Regional Research.* Vol. 37, No. 5, pp. 1707–1723.

Shin, J. (2015). Car-free zone street...occupied by the cars [online]. Translated from Korean. *Chungcheongilbo.* Updated 26 January 2016. 19:34:36. [Viewed 25 March 2017]. Available from: http://m.ccdailynews.com/news/articleView.html?idxno=858139

Song, K. (2010). Study on analysing the problems of urban improvement projects and the system for urban regeneration. *Architectural Institute of Korea.* Vol. 26, Issue 1, pp. 307 – 314.

Tallon, A. (2010). *Urban Regeneration in the UK.* Routledge.

Throsby, D. (2010). *The Economics of Cultural Policy.* Cambridge University Press.

Timur, S. and Getz, D. (2008). *Sustainable tourism development: how do destination stakeholders perceive sustainable urban tourism?.* Vol. 17, Issue 4.

Yeonhap news (2016). Culture-led regeneration could not be given up... the controversial issue on the formal Tobacco Factory in Cheongju [online]. Translated from Korean. *Yeonhap News.* Updated 26 October 2016. 11:29. [Viewed 20 March 2017]. Available from: http://www.yonhapnews.co.kr/bulletin/2016/10/26/0200000000AKR20161026078700064.HTML?input=1195m

Yokohama Joint Statement. (2014). *Yokohama Joint Statement* [online]. Available from: http://file.tcs-asia.org/file_manager/files/tcs/6.%20Human%20and%20 Cultural%20Exchange/1.%20English/1.%20Culture/(2014.12.30)%20Yokohama %20Joint%20Statement%20of%20the%20Sixth%20Trilateral%20Culture%20Min isters%E2%80%99%20Meeting.pdf

Yoo, S. (2016). Cheongju, continues with Culture City of East Asia exchange projects this year [online]. *Chungbuk Newspaper.* Updated Available at: 23 February 2016, 18:22. [Viewed 17 October 2016]. Available from: http://www.inews365.com/news/article.html?no=435630

Yoon, B. and Nam, J. (2015). *The Analysis on Socio-Economic Ripple Effect of Project for Urban Regeneration.* Korea Planners Association. Vol. 50, Issue 8, pp. 19-38.

Yu, B. (2013). A Study on the Legislative Process of the 'Urban Regeneration and Assistance Act'. Korea Planners Association. Vol. 48, Issue 6, pp. 367-385.

Yu, D. (2012). How the Hanok village became the Hanok village? [online]. Translated from Korean. *Cultplay blog.* Updated 4 December 2012. 13:53. [Viewed 20 March 2017]. Available from: http://cultplay.egloos.com/5700138

Yudice, G. (2003). *The Expediency of Culture: Uses of Culture in the Global Era.* Duke University Press.

Vickery, J. (2007). *The Emergence of Culture-led Regeneration: A policy concept and its discontents.* Centre for Cultural Policy Studies.

*Presenters at the seminars and conferences in South Korea (Their opinions are mentioned and explained in Chapter 4)

Ahn, J. S. (2015). Professor at university.

Hong, M. Y. (2015). Head of urban architecture company.

Hwang, H. Y. (2015). Professor at university.

Jung, C. M. (2015). Professor at university.

Kim, J. Y. (2015a). Researcher.

Kim, Y. J. (2015b). Researcher for culture and tourism.

Koo, J. H. (2015). Professor at university.

Kwon, Y. R. (2015). Head of culture consulting company.

Index

www.ingramcontent.com/pod-product-compliance
Lightning Source LLC
Chambersburg PA
CBHW062041270326
41929CB00014B/2490